P9-BZS-117

Lights, Camera, Hairballs!

GARFIELD AT THE MOVIES

Lights, Camera, Hairballs!

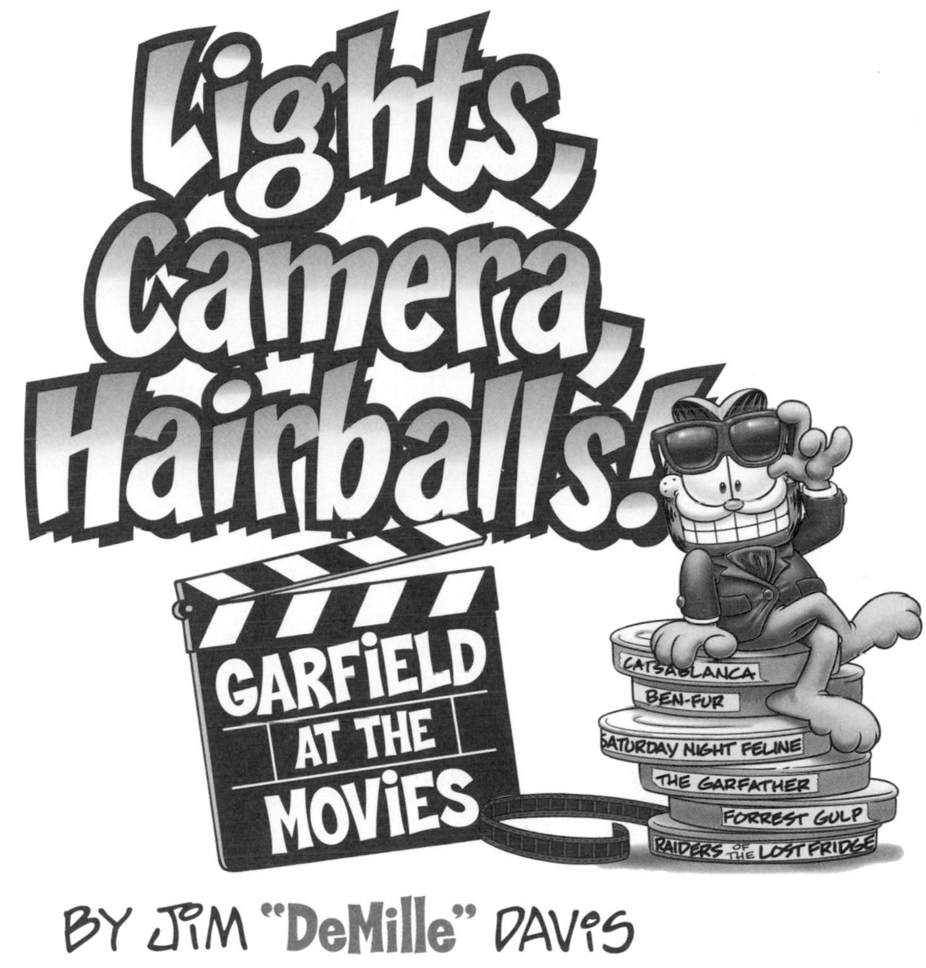
GARFIELD
AT THE
MOVIES
CATSABLANCA
BEN-FUR
SATURDAY NIGHT FELINE
THE GARFATHER
FORREST GULP
RAIDERS OF THE LOST FRIDGE

BY JIM "DeMille" DAVIS

with

Mark "Scorsese" Acey
Scott "von Stroheim" Nickel
Brett "Corman" Koth
Thomas "Hitchcock" Howard

Ballantine Books • New York

A Ballantine Books Trade Paperback Original

Copyright © 2006 by PAWS, Inc. All rights reserved.
"GARFIELD" and the GARFIELD characters are trademarks of PAWS, Inc.

Published in the United States by Ballantine Books, an imprint of The Random House Publishing Group, a division of Random House, Inc., New York.

BALLANTINE and colophon are registered trademarks of Random House, Inc.

Product, company, and character names may be trademarks of their respective companies.

The movie images and content contained in this work are from *Garfield the Movie*, and the Garfield theatrical movie sequel, TM and © Twentieth Century Fox Film Corporation. All rights reserved.

ISBN 0-345-49134-3

Printed in the United States of America

www.ballantinebooks.com

9 8 7 6 5 4 3 2 1

EDITORIAL
Mark Acey, Scott Nickel, and Brett Koth

ART DIRECTION
Betsy Knotts

DESIGN
Thomas Howard

ILLUSTRATION
Gary Barker, Lori Barker, Jamie Crawford, Larry Fentz,
Mike Fentz, Thomas Howard, Brett Koth, Dave Kuhn,
Lynette Nuding, Eric Reaves, and Glenn Zimmerman

PRODUCTION
Jon Barnard, Linda Duell, Kenny Goetzinger, Brad Hill, and Betsy Knotts

PHOTOGRAPHY
Gemma La Mana

COMING ATTRACTIONS

INTRODUCTION

Baseball was once called our "national pastime." But, in reality, it's movies that have been captivating the imaginations and capturing the hearts of Americans—including my own—ever since the first moving images flickered on the big screen.

Men and women, young and old, cool cats, even dumb dogs . . . we all love the movies. Whether watched in theaters or at home, movies provide countless hours of entertainment and enjoyment (and buckets of popcorn!) all over the world, every day of the year. Yeah, baby . . . that's movie mojo!

I know I'm a big fat film fanatic: that's why I decided to write this book. For the most part, it's a tribute to Tinseltown and classic movies of every genre. However, when Hollywood hacks up a hairball, I point that out, too.

But I'm not just a fan and a critic: I'm also a movie star! (Hey, if Madonna can act, so can I.) That's why I devoted a small section to my own films. Like I always say, "If you don't indulge yourself, who will?"

But enough with the trailer . . .
IT'S SHOWTIME!

ACTION/ADVENTURE

Panel 1: I RENTED A VIDEO, GARFIELD

Panel 2: IT HAS EVERYTHING! ACTION, ADVENTURE...

Panel 3: AND A GREAT SOUND TRACK! — "THE POLKA NINJAS"

Fast cars. Cool gadgets. Big explosions. Now, that's entertainment! Who needs deep psychological drama and insightful dialogue when you can have Jackie Chan kung-fuing his way through a hundred guys?

Appreciating action movies is definitely a "guy thing." We don't expect women to understand it. We don't understand their movies, either. We just want to be left alone with our popcorn and Junior Mints to enjoy some extremely loud, mindless fun. We don't want to watch anything about traveling pants or people falling in love—unless they're doing it in a speeding car or while fighting an army of Orcs.

The only thing I don't like about action movies is the aging action star. What's up with all these old geezers?

Sean Connery and Clint Eastwood should be less worried about getting zapped by the bad guy and more worried about breaking a hip.

Maybe Hollywood can solve this problem by popping an aging actor's head onto a CG body. It's really not much of a stretch when you think about it. Arnold Schwarzenegger and Sylvester Stallone are practically cartoon characters anyway.

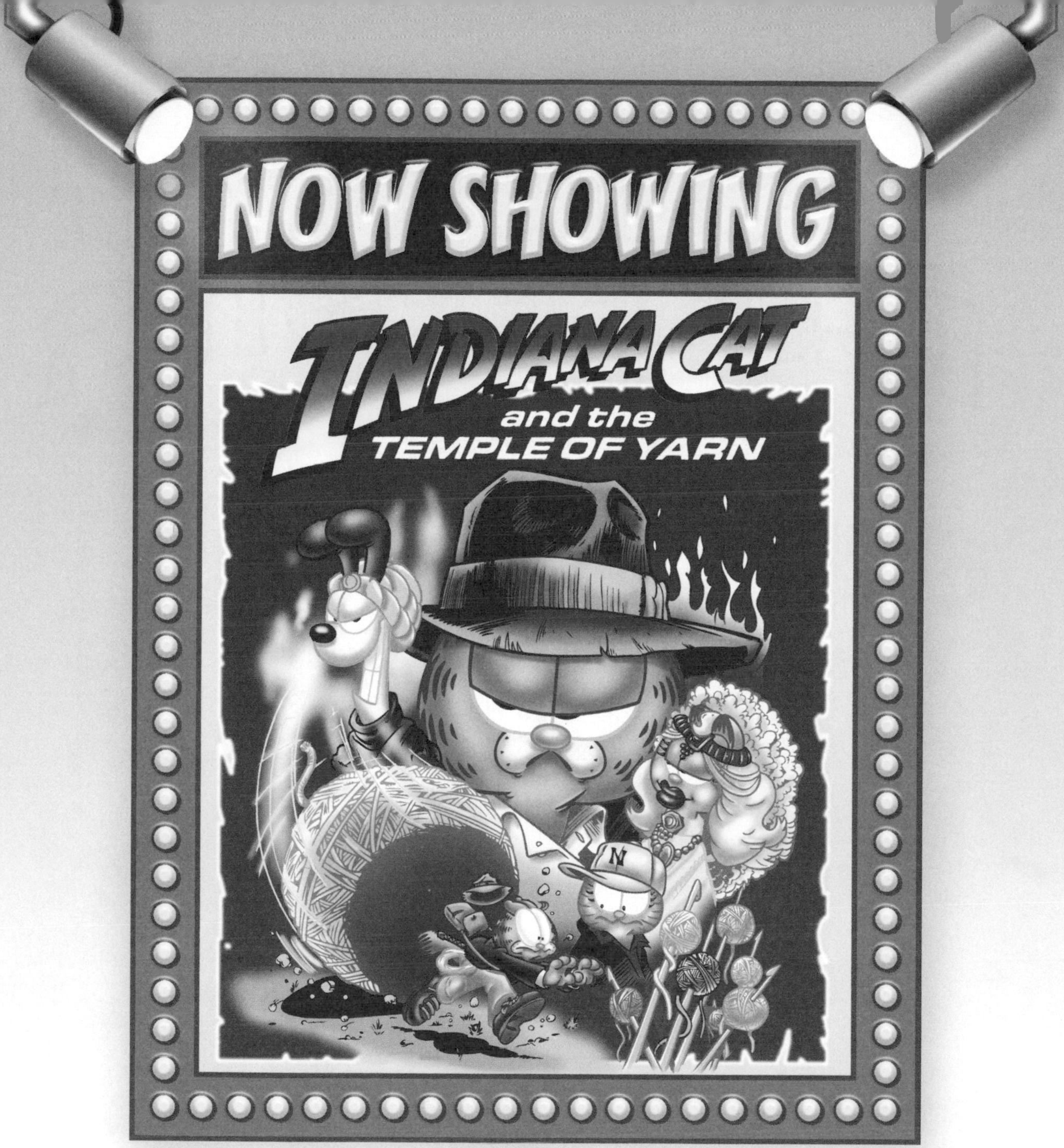
NOW SHOWING
INDIANA CAT
and the
TEMPLE OF YARN
N

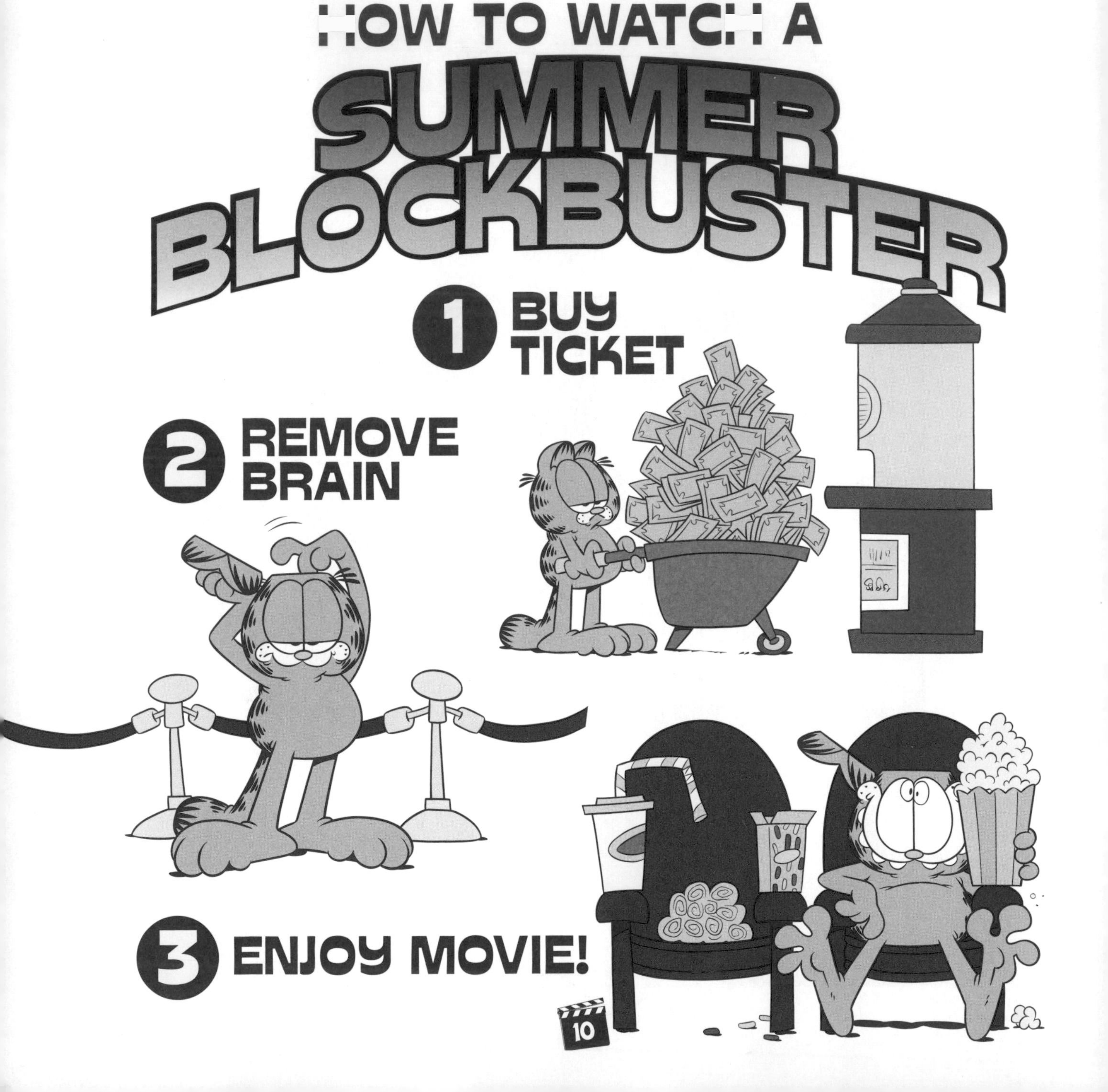
HOW TO WATCH A
SUMMER BLOCKBUSTER
1 BUY TICKET
2 REMOVE BRAIN
3 ENJOY MOVIE!

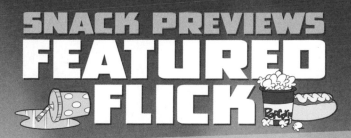

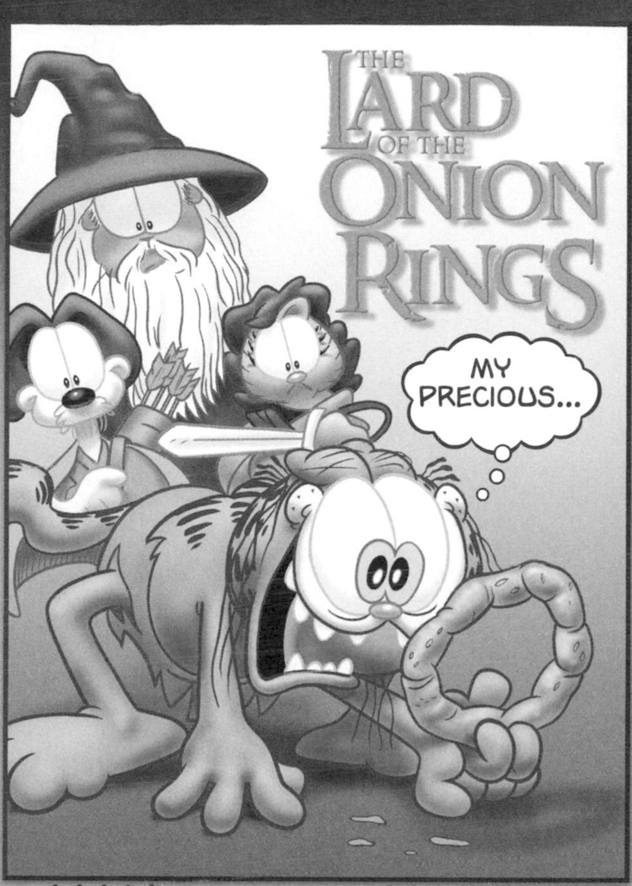
THE
LARD
OF THE
ONION
RINGS
MY PRECIOUS...

A visual slice of heaven A "reel" treat
Worth a taste Barely palatable Gagger

SNACK PREVIEWS FEATURED FLICK

THE GOOD:
Lots of action, lots of magic, and lots of fried foods!

THE BAD:
Three-hour movie = bursting bladder.

THE SCORE:

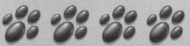

"Made me hungry for the sequels."

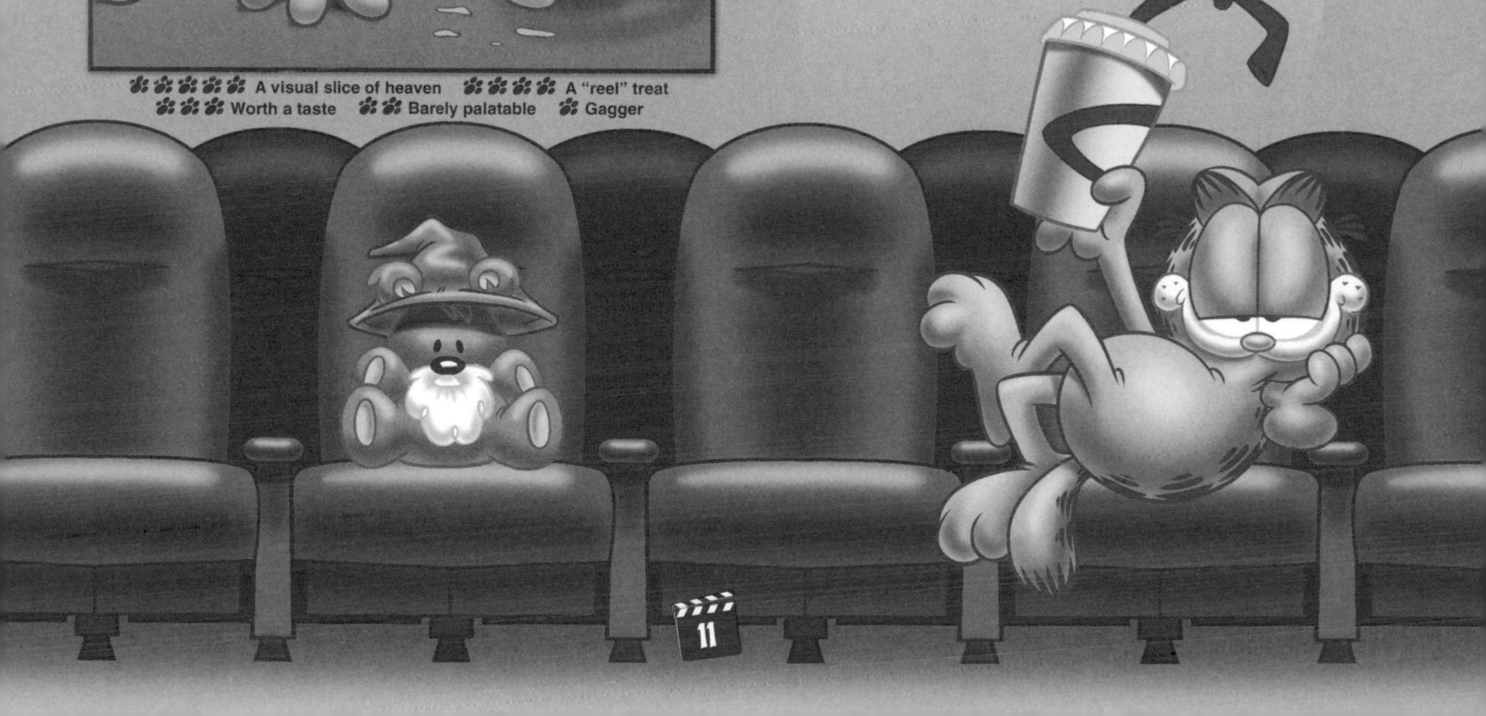

Animated

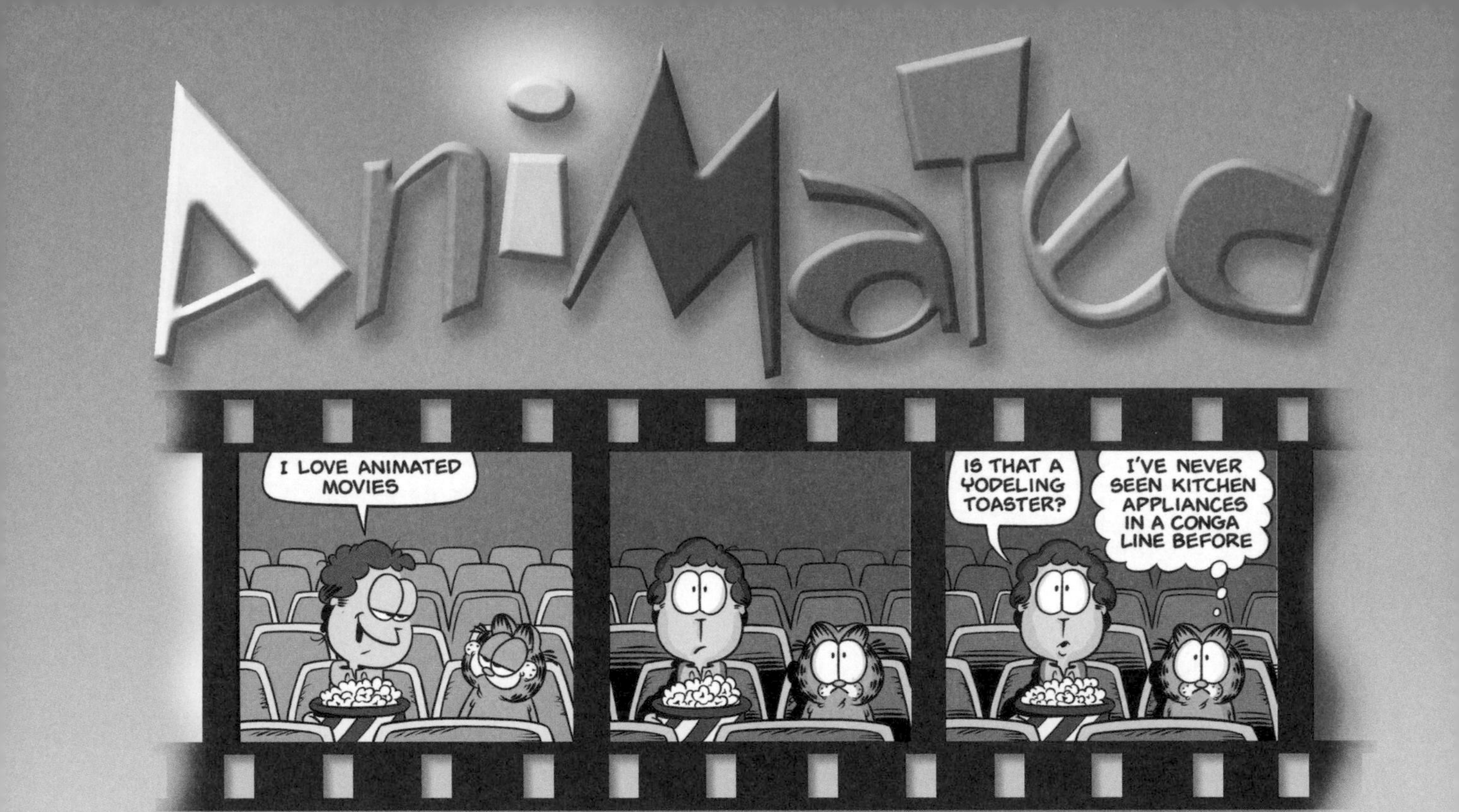

I LOVE ANIMATED MOVIES
IS THAT A YODELING TOASTER?
I'VE NEVER SEEN KITCHEN APPLIANCES IN A CONGA LINE BEFORE

In 1928 the world was introduced to a little talking mouse named Mickey. Fifty years later a wisecracking orange cat with a taste for lasagna came on the scene. The squeaky-voiced rodent may have seniority, but I'm the real cartoon king. In fact, I have more personality in my little paw than Mickey and his whole goofy menagerie (no pun intended) combined.

But enough cattiness. Let's talk 'toons. Over the years, cartoons have been criticized as mindless entertainment. Sure, they're not Shakespeare, but come on—is there anything funnier than someone getting hit on the head with a giant anvil? Or run over by a steamroller? I say if you don't laugh at that, *you're* the one who's brain-dead.

Luckily, animation is getting a lot more respect these days. Disney's *Beauty and the Beast* was even nominated for the Best Picture Academy Award in 1991. (I think my version—*Beauty and the Feast*—would've clinched the Oscar®. But I digress.)

Who are my favorite cartoon stars? I like Nemo (with a little tartar sauce), Bambi (mmm, venison!), and, of course, the great Bugs Bunny (Wabbit Stew, anyone?).

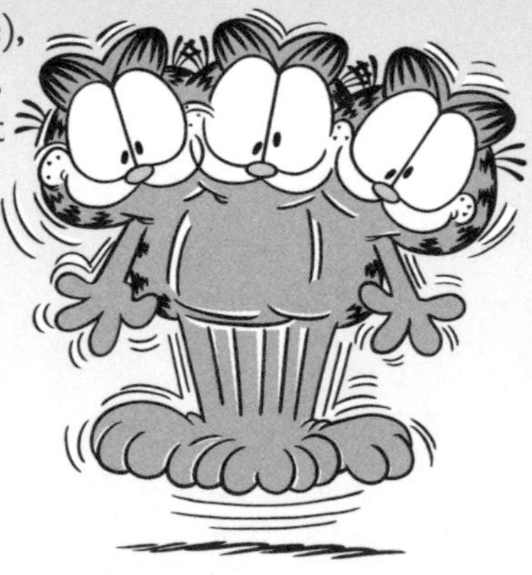

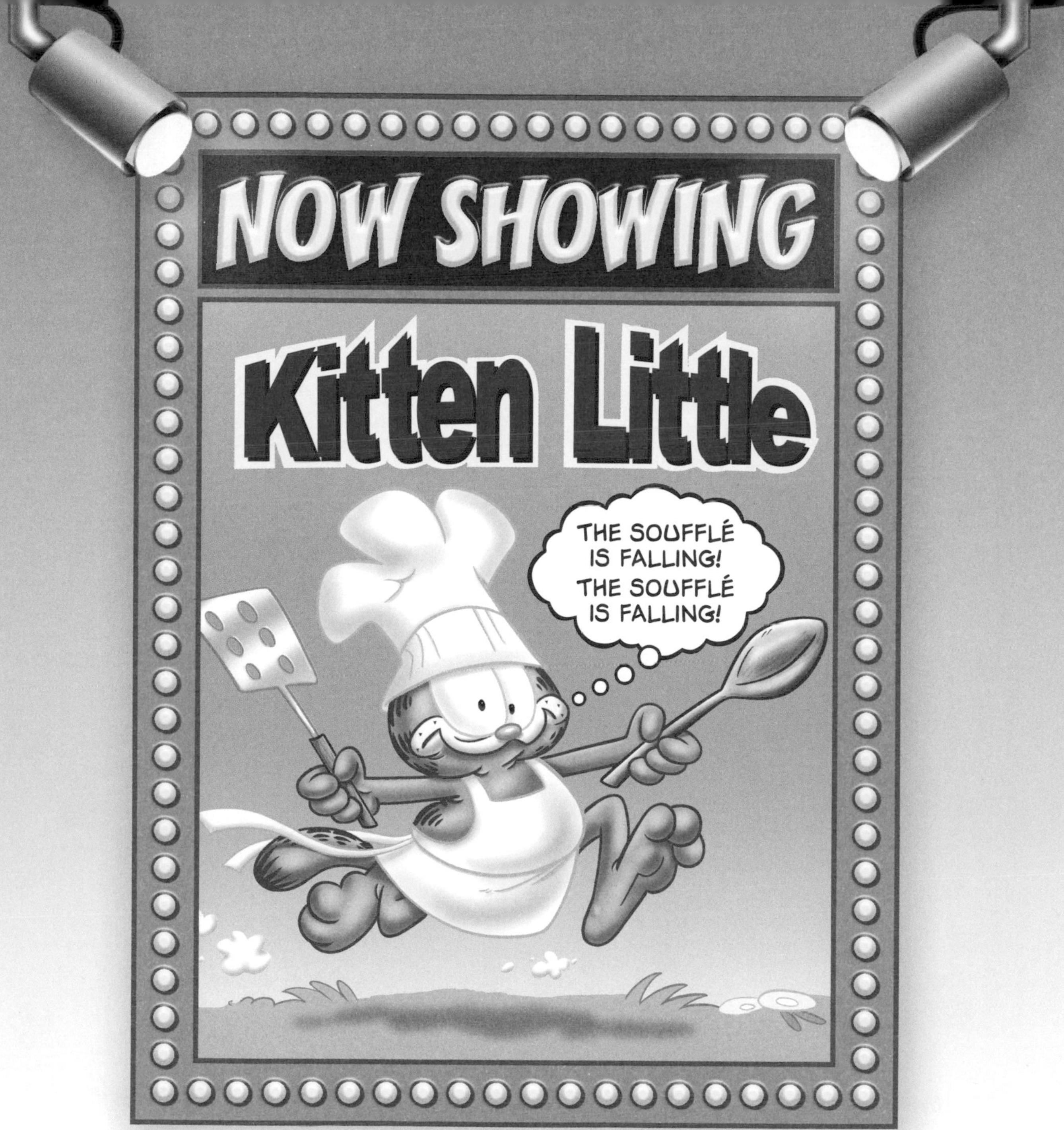
NOW SHOWING
Kitten Little
THE SOUFFLÉ IS FALLING! THE SOUFFLÉ IS FALLING!

CARTOON PHYSICS

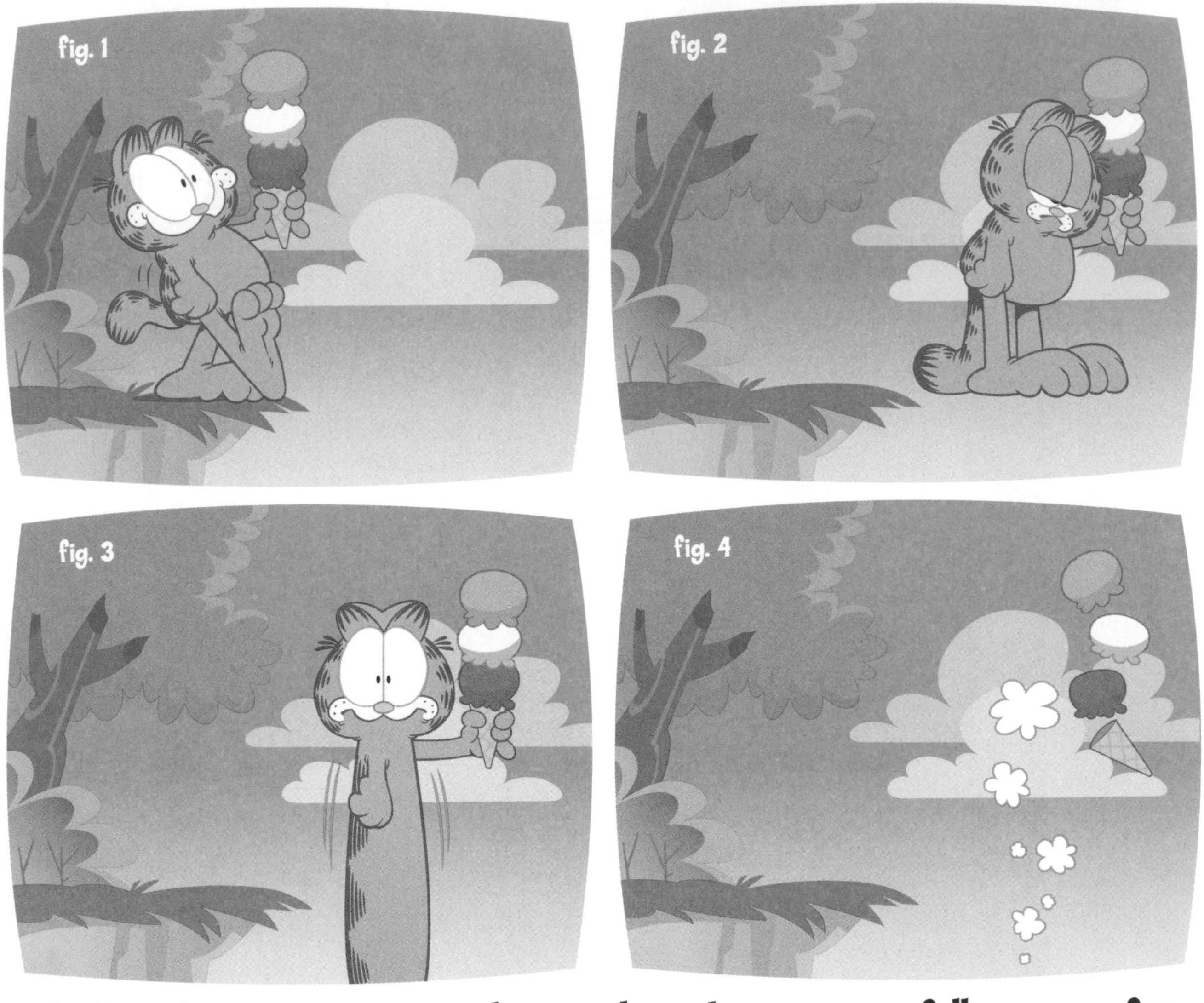
fig. 1
fig. 2
fig. 3
fig. 4

The law of gravity never applies until one becomes painfully aware of it.

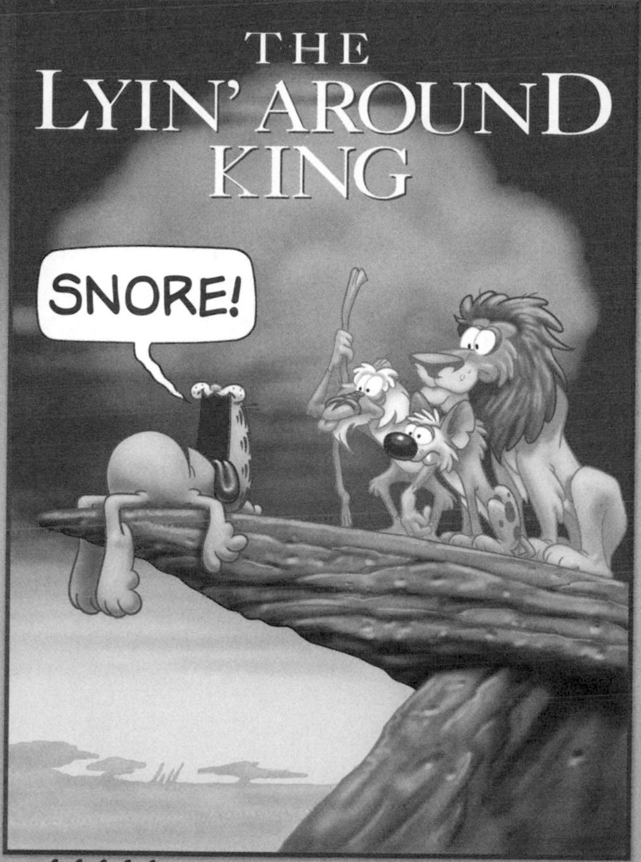
THE LYIN' AROUND KING
SNORE!

🐾🐾🐾🐾🐾 A visual slice of heaven 🐾🐾🐾🐾 A "reel" treat
🐾🐾🐾 Worth a taste 🐾🐾 Barely palatable 🐾 Gagger

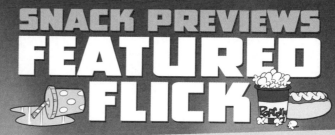

SNACK PREVIEWS FEATURED FLICK

THE GOOD:
Meercat and warthog steal the show from snoozing star.

THE BAD:
Inane songs still stuck in my head.

THE SCORE:
🐾

"A sure cure for insomnia."

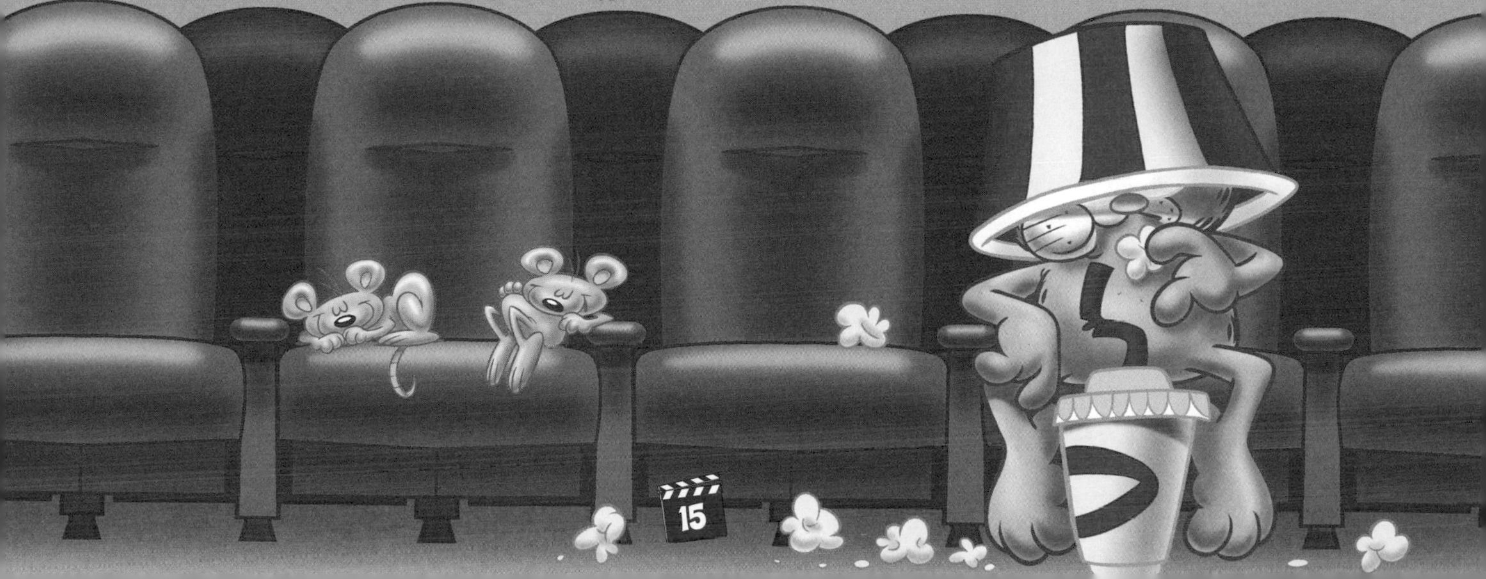

CLASSICS

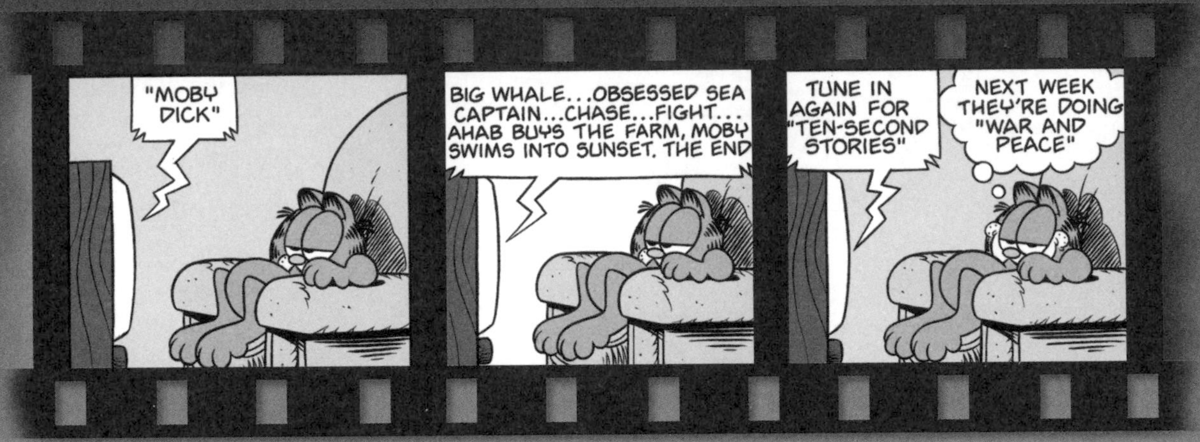
"MOBY DICK"
BIG WHALE...OBSESSED SEA CAPTAIN...CHASE...FIGHT... AHAB BUYS THE FARM, MOBY SWIMS INTO SUNSET. THE END
TUNE IN AGAIN FOR "TEN-SECOND STORIES"
NEXT WEEK THEY'RE DOING "WAR AND PEACE"

There's no movie like an old movie. Back in the day, Hollywood really knew how to make 'em. Not that current films are all bad. It's just that when you compare, say, *Citizen Kane* to *Dude, Where's My Car?* there's really no comparison.

But classics don't have to be old. There are plenty of recent films that make the grade: *The Graduate, One Flew Over the Cuckoo's Nest, Taxi Driver, American Beauty,* and, of course, *Garfield: The Movie* (but more about that starting on page 82!).

Classics can be in any genre, from drama to comedy—even documentary (okay, maybe that's a stretch). What makes a classic a classic? That's like asking what makes lasagna nature's most perfect food. It's not the ingredients; it's how they're prepared. Sometimes you mix everything together and you get *Gone With the Wind*; sometimes you get *Gigli.*

We all have our favorite scene from our favorite classic: "Rosebud" from *Citizen Kane*; the shower scene from Hitchcock's *Psycho*; the horse's head from *The Godfather*; the mashed potato scene from *Close Encounters of the Third Kind* (always makes me hungry!).

On the next few pages, I offer my own unique take on a few of the finer films to grace the silver screen. . . .

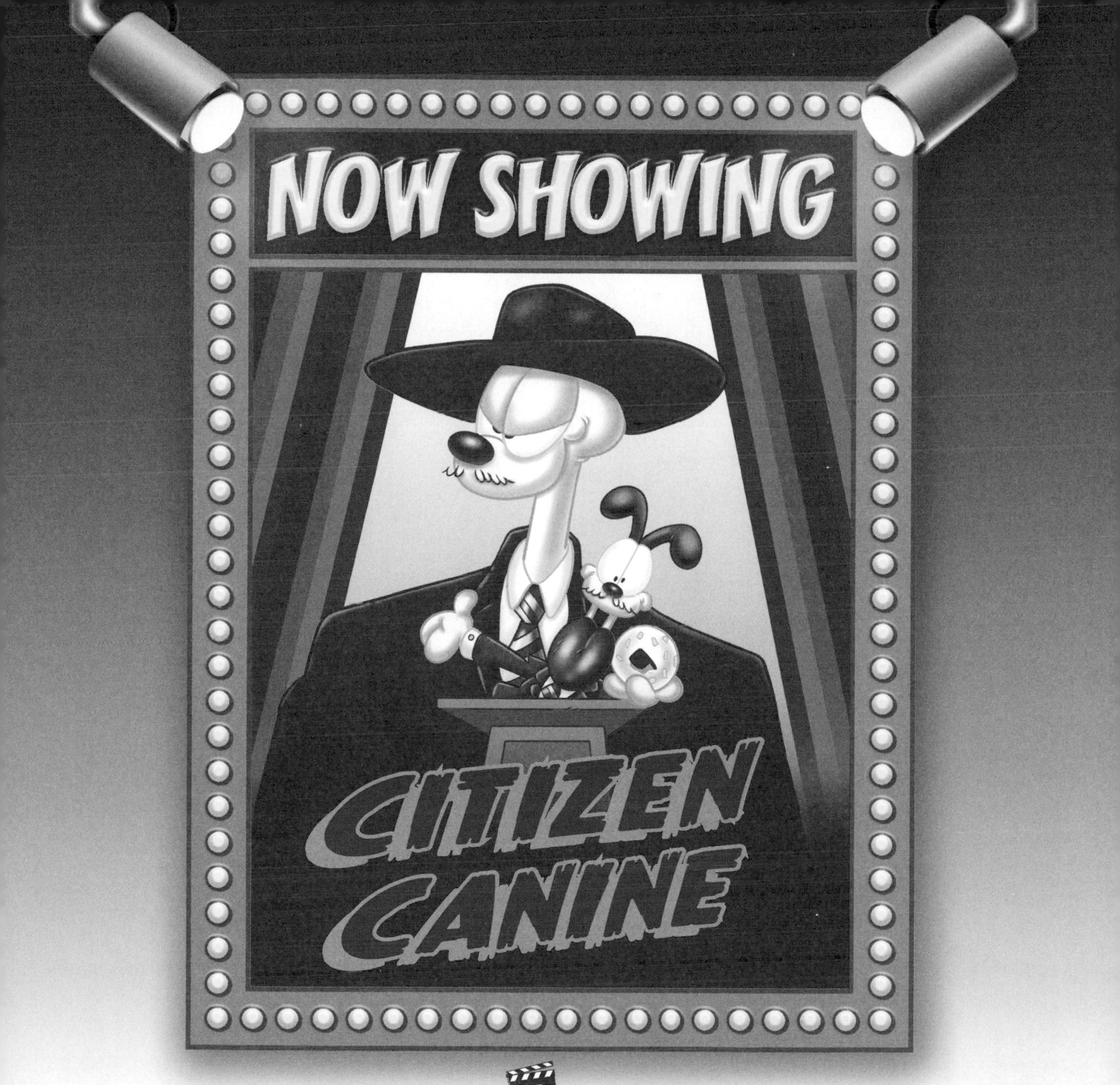
NOW SHOWING
CITIZEN
CANINE

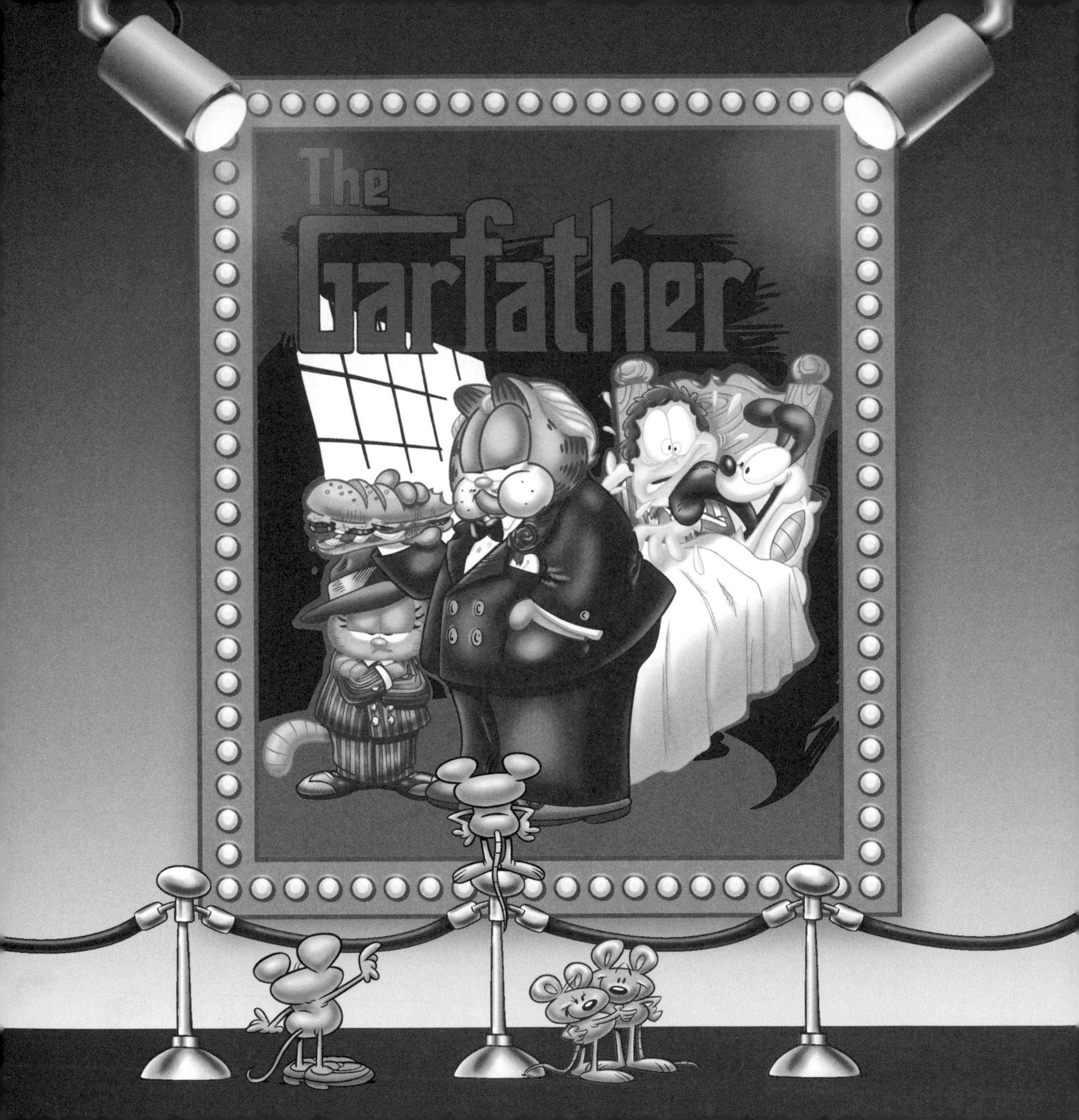
The Garfather

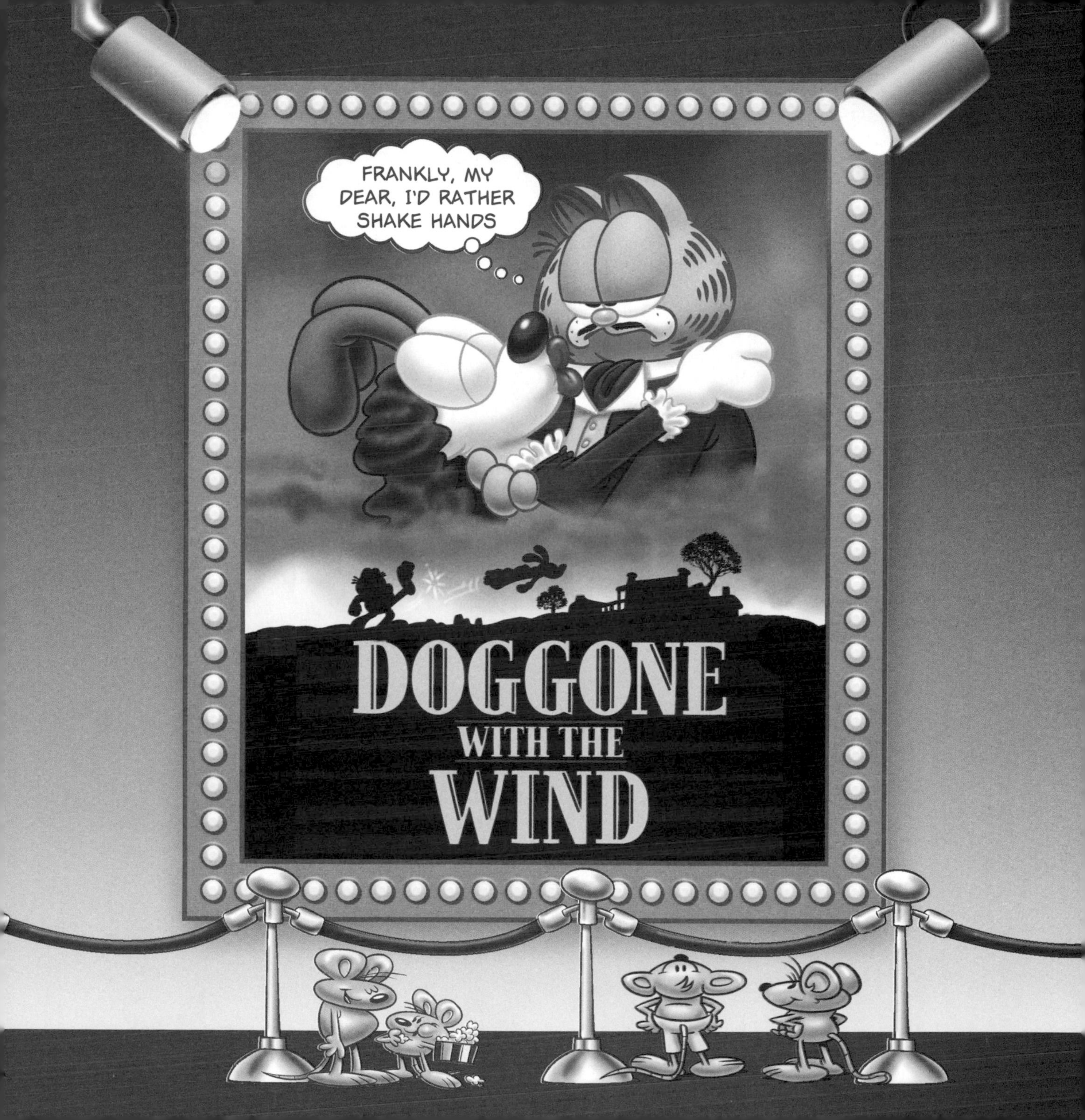
FRANKLY, MY DEAR, I'D RATHER SHAKE HANDS
DOGGONE WITH THE WIND

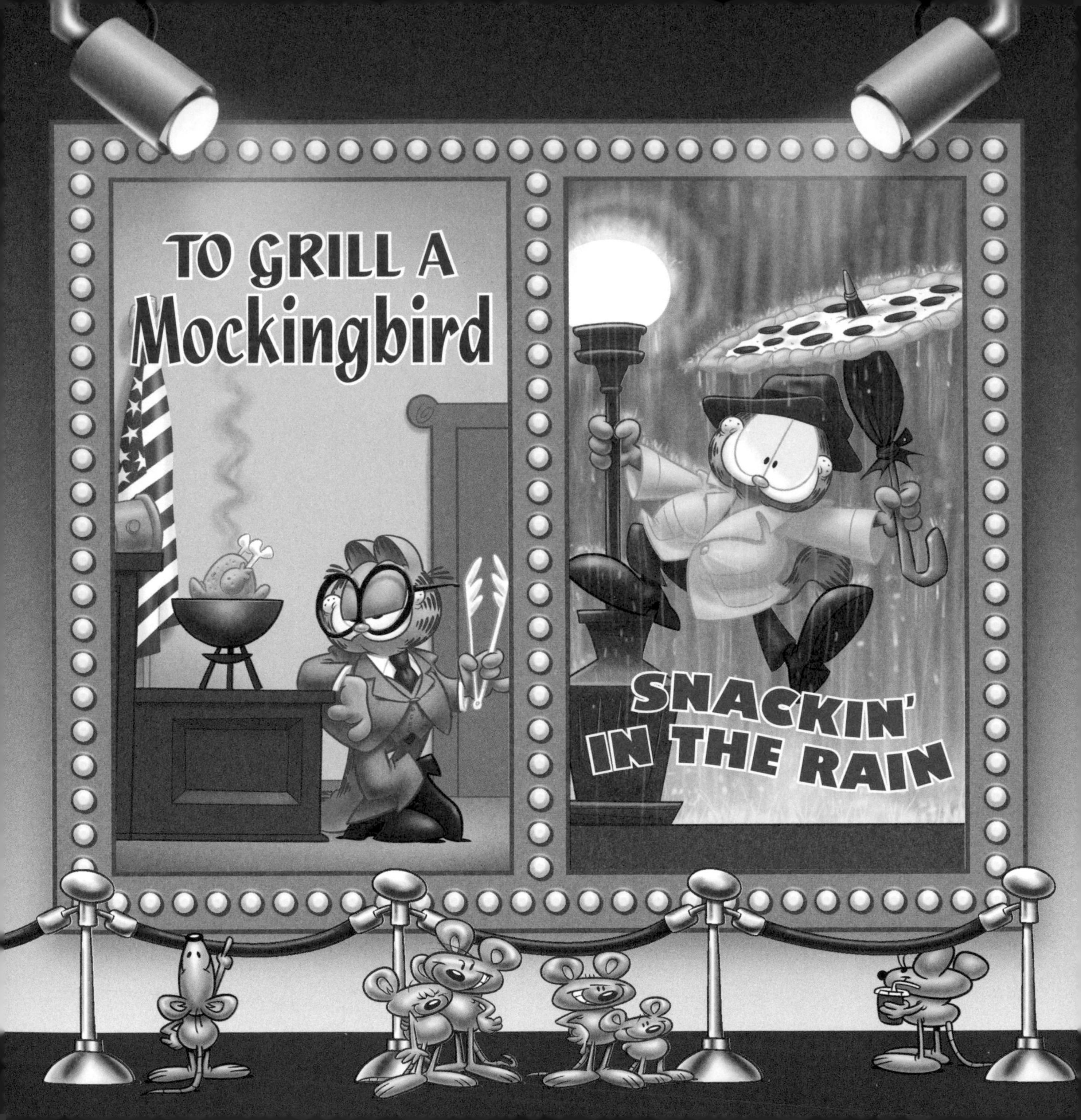
TO GRILL A
Mockingbird
SNACKIN'
IN THE RAIN

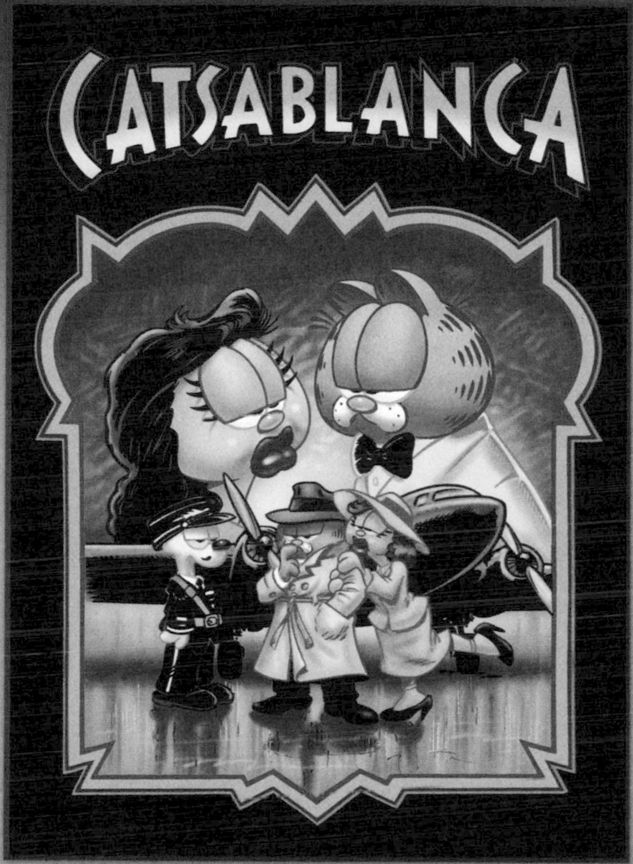
CATSABLANCA

Paw-print ratings key (each rating below is shown by its number of paw prints, from five down to one):

5 paws: A visual slice of heaven
4 paws: A "reel" treat
3 paws: Worth a taste
2 paws: Barely palatable
1 paw: Gagger

SNACK PREVIEWS
FEATURED FLICK

THE GOOD:
A story of love, honor, sacrifice, and courage that just keeps getting better as time goes by.

THE BAD:
Say something against this film and you'll regret it. Maybe not now, but soon, and for the rest of your life.

THE SCORE:

(Five paw prints.)

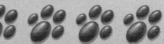

"Play it again, Sam! I've got a big appetite for the classics."

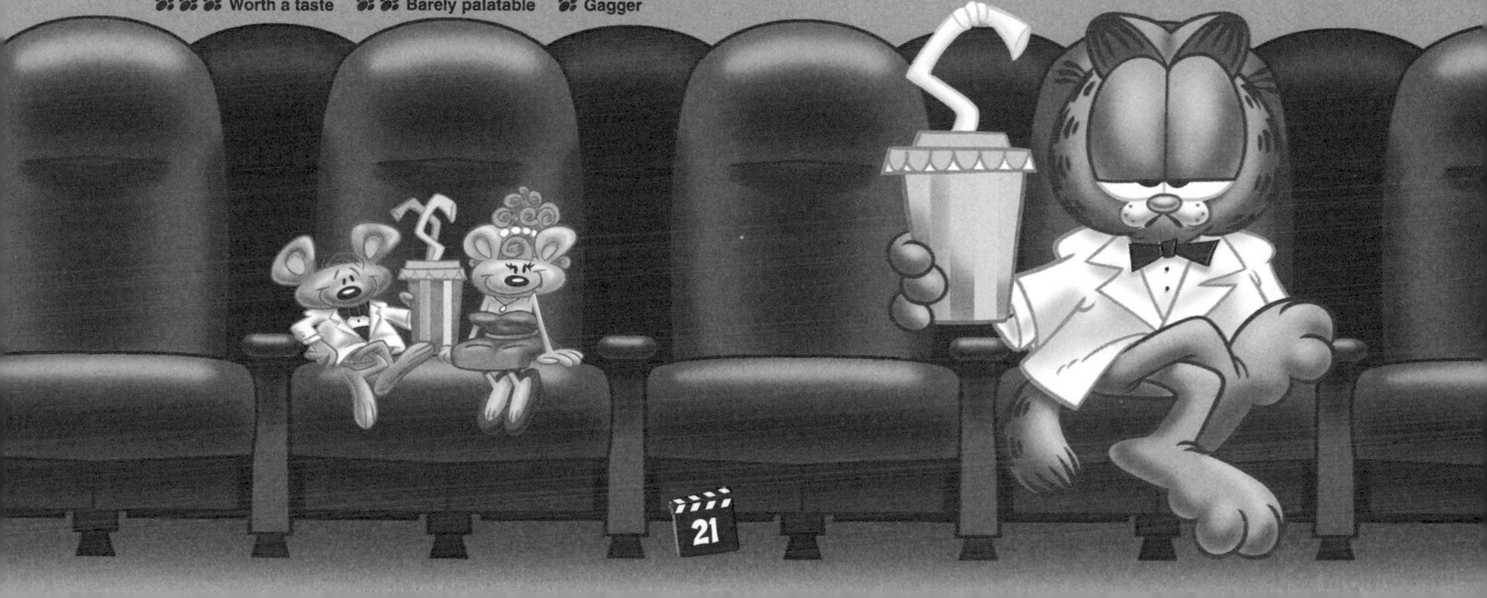

GARFIELD'S Classic Movie Lines...

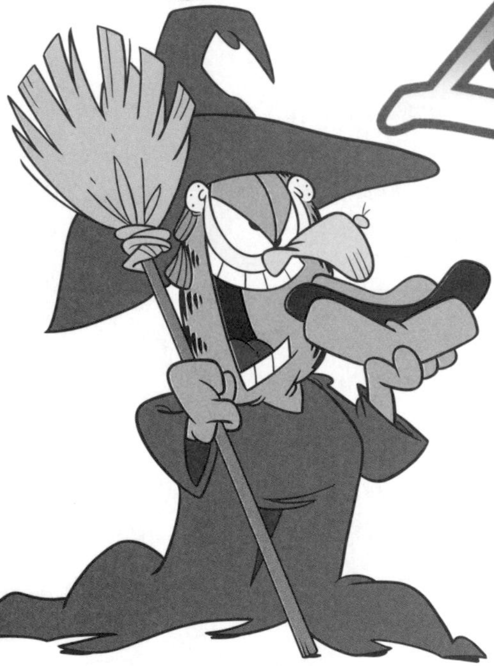

"I'll get you, my pretty, and your hot dog, too!"

—*The Wizard of Paws*

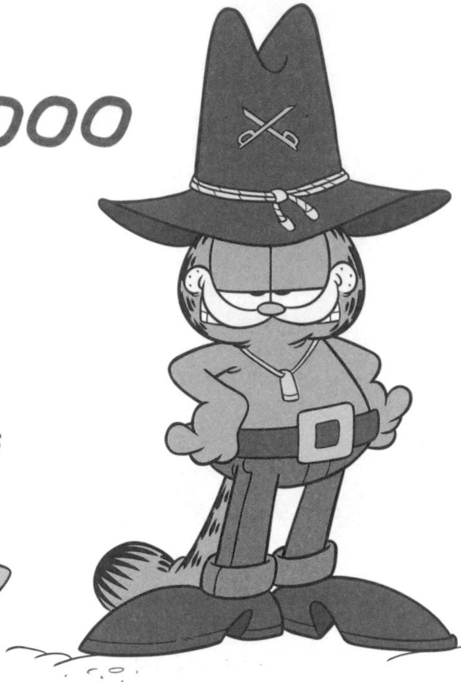

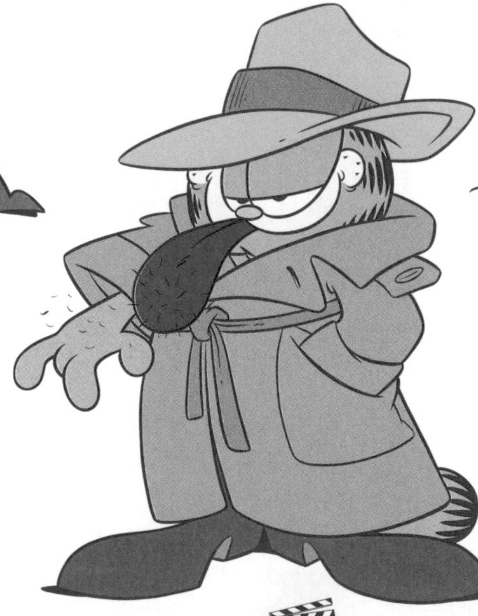

"HERE'S LICKING AT YOU, KID."

—*Catsablanca*

"I love the smell of jerk chicken in the morning."

—*Apocalypso Now*

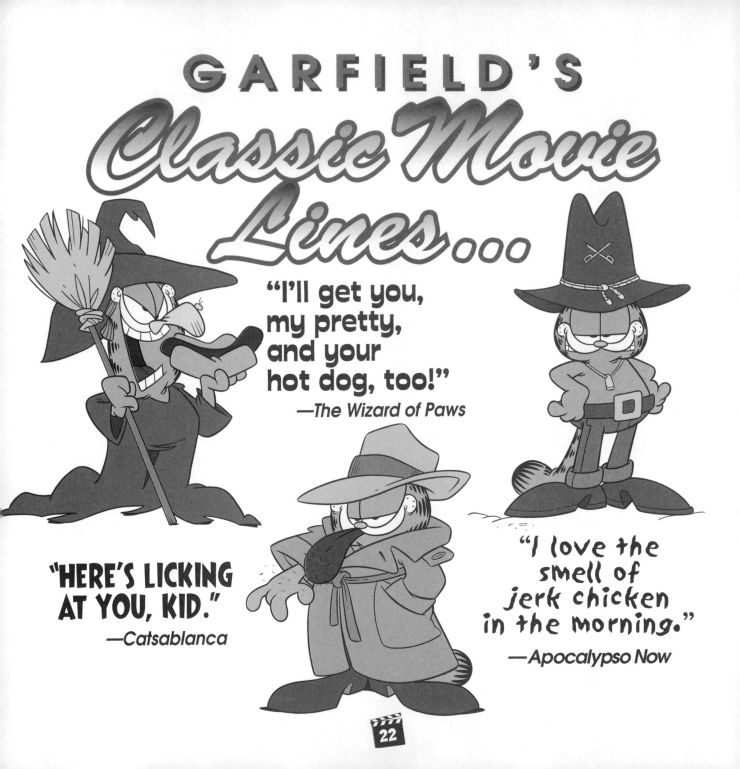

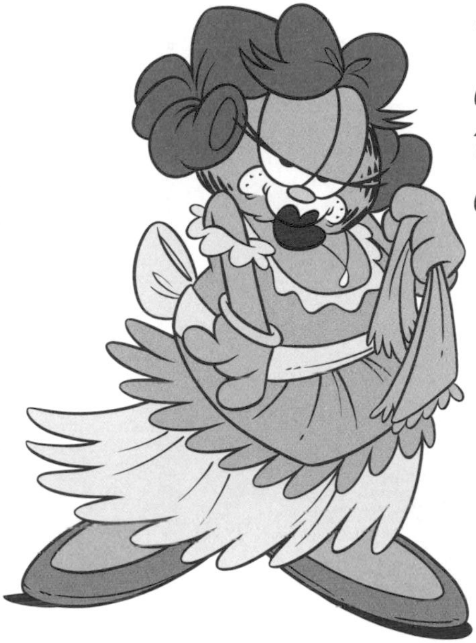

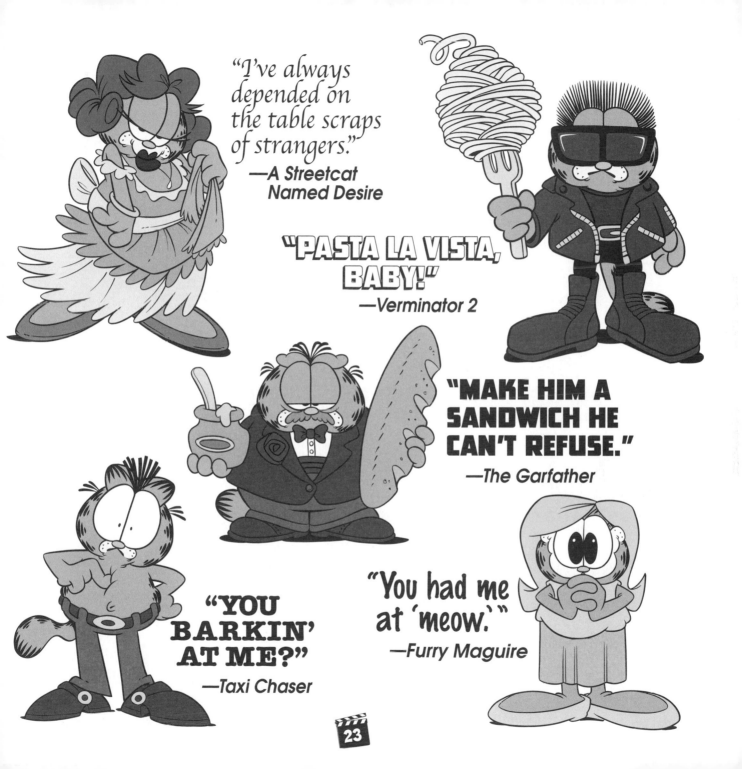

"I've always depended on the table scraps of strangers."

—*A Streetcat Named Desire*

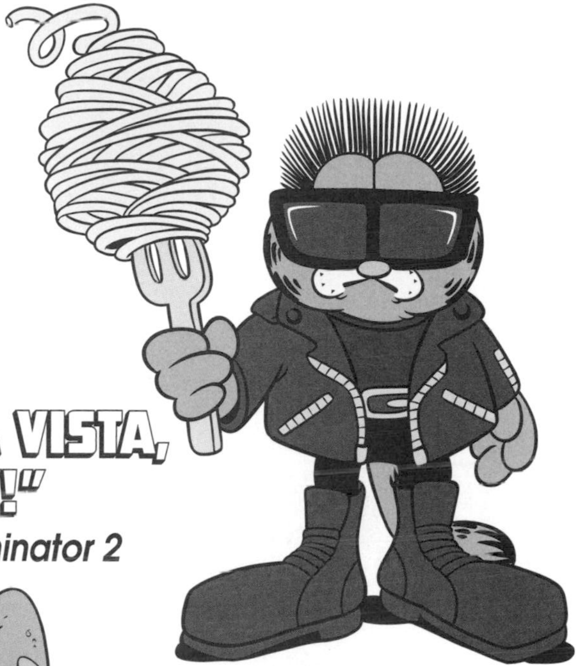

"PASTA LA VISTA, BABY!"

—*Verminator 2*

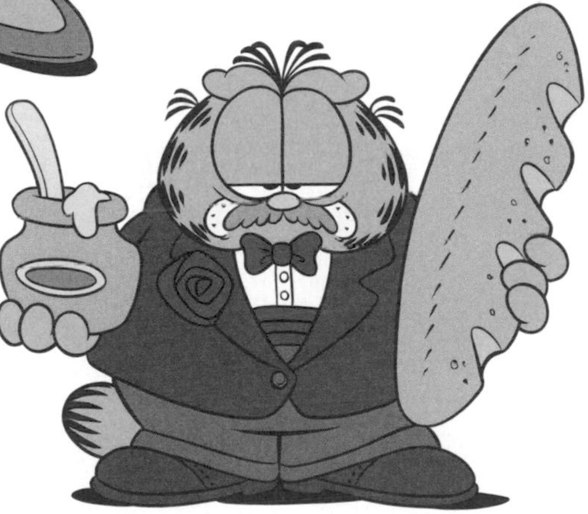

"MAKE HIM A SANDWICH HE CAN'T REFUSE."

—*The Garfather*

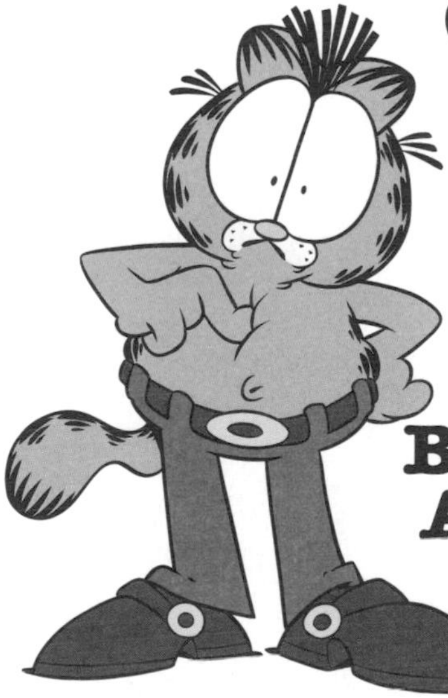

"YOU BARKIN' AT ME?"

—*Taxi Chaser*

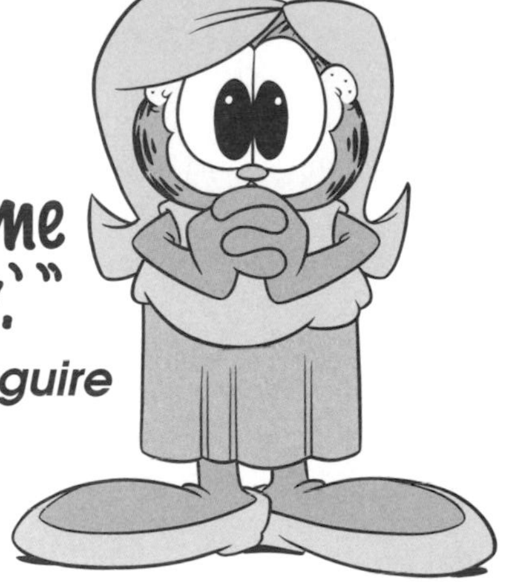

"You had me at 'meow.'"

—*Furry Maguire*

COMEDY

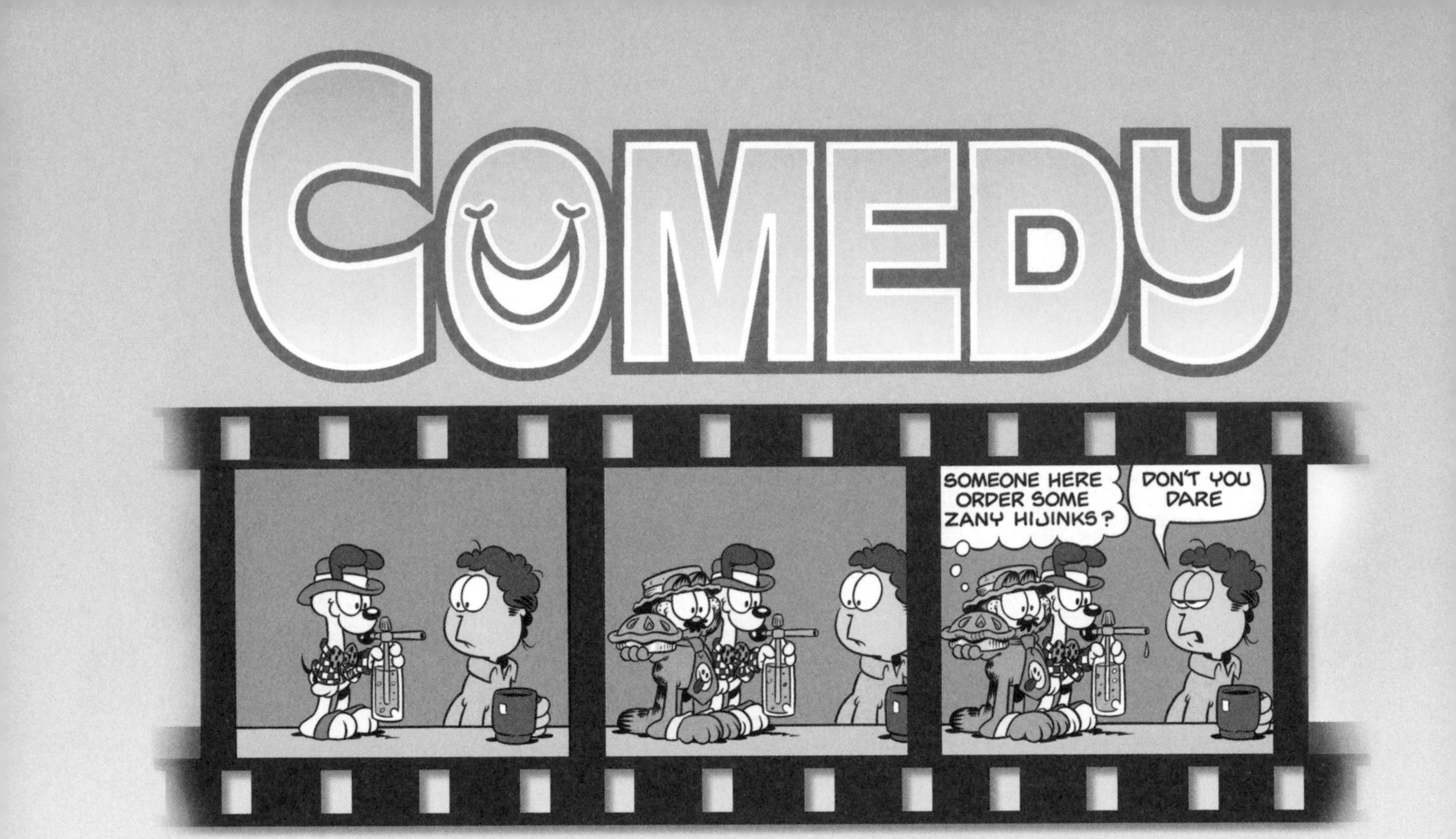
SOMEONE HERE ORDER SOME ZANY HIJINKS?
DON'T YOU DARE

The famous quotation "Dying is easy. Comedy is hard" has been attributed to various people. While there may be uncertainty over the source, there's no doubt in my mind that the sentiment is true. (Of course, that's easy for me to say: I have *nine* lives.)

When it comes to movies, dramas hog the Oscars: It's extremely difficult for comedies to take home the hardware. But while dramas win the awards, it's comedies that people really love, because people love to laugh. Let's face it: Given a choice between *Citizen Kane* and *Weekend at Bernie's*, most viewers will opt for the "humor" of dead bodies waterskiing. That's the wacky, if tacky, truth of the human condition.

The top two spots on the American Film Institute list of the 100 funniest films are *Some Like It Hot* and *Tootsie*. Obviously, guys in drag are funny; I know I like it. I also like the physical comedy of The Three Stooges and the snappy dialogue of Groucho Marx and Woody Allen in their movies. These "yukmeisters" don't just amuse me; they *inspire* me. Hmm, I think I'll give Odie a swift kick, followed by a verbal shot. That always tickles my funny bone.

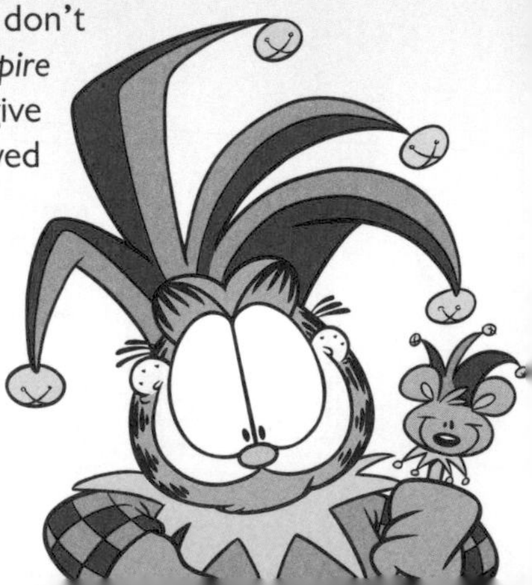

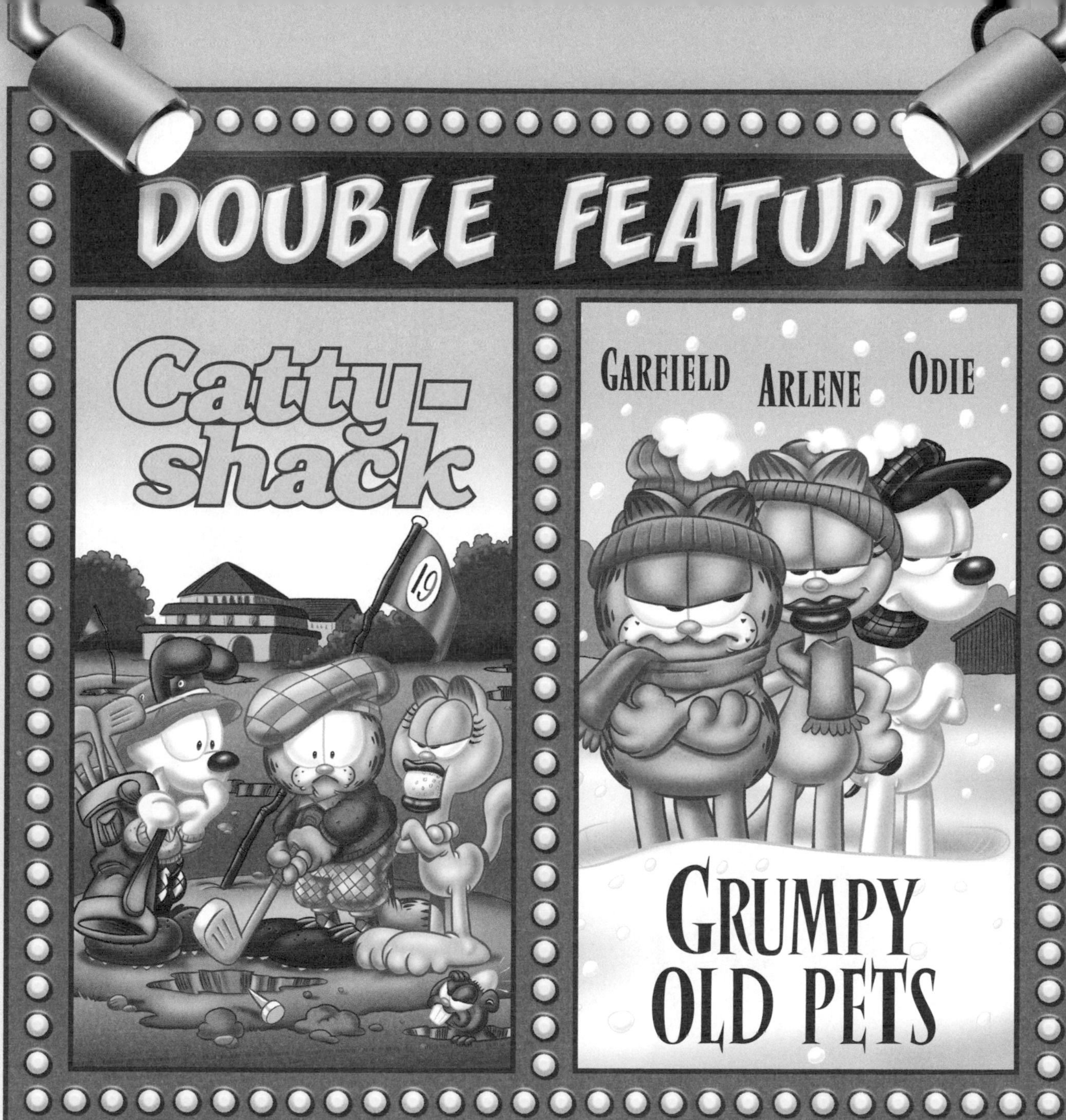
DOUBLE FEATURE
Catty-shack
19
GARFIELD
ARLENE
ODIE
GRUMPY OLD PETS

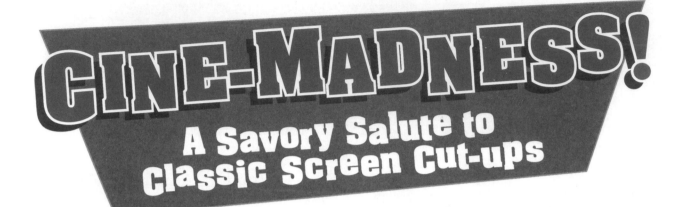

CINE-MADNESS!

A Savory Salute to Classic Screen Cut-ups

"Garfo Marx" in DUCK SOUP AND SANDWICHES

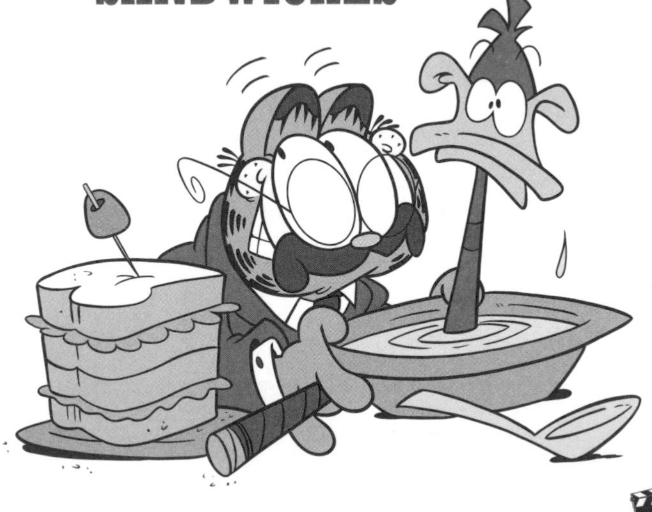

"W. C. Garfields" in MY LITTLE FRICASSEE

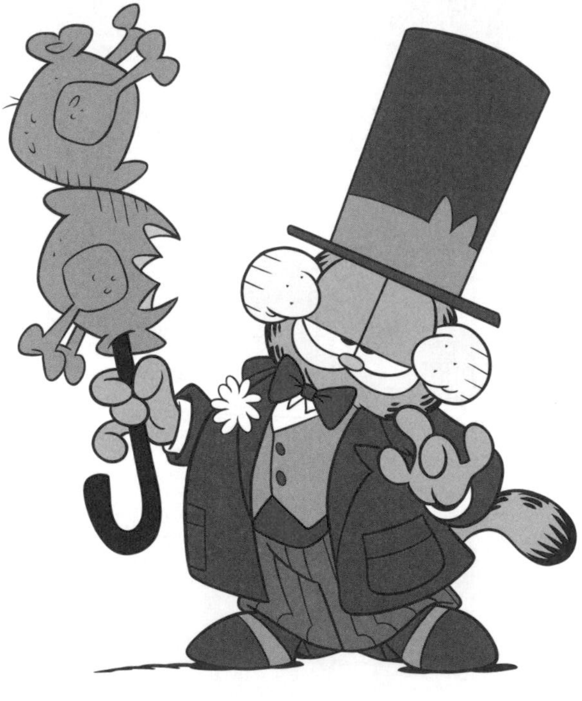

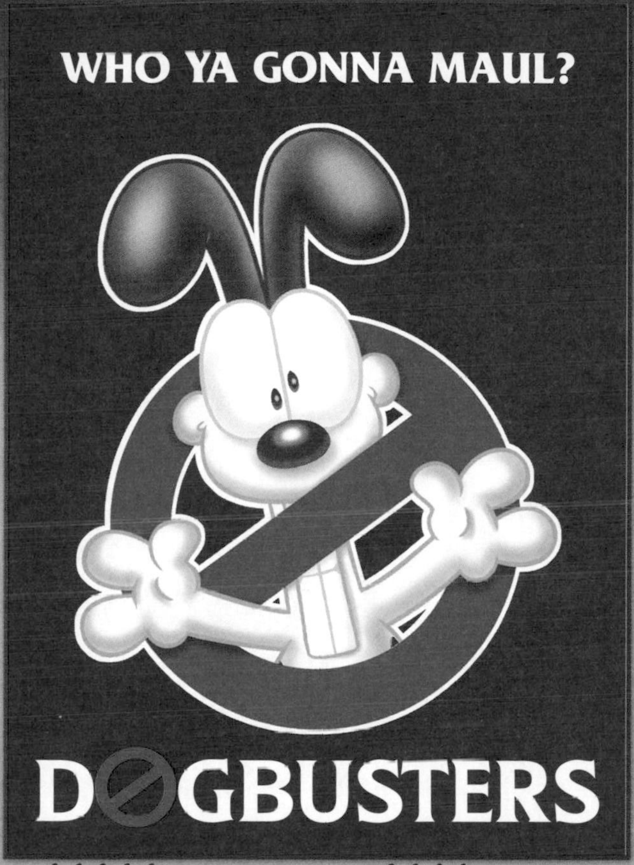
WHO YA GONNA MAUL?
DOGBUSTERS

SNACK PREVIEWS FEATURED FLICK

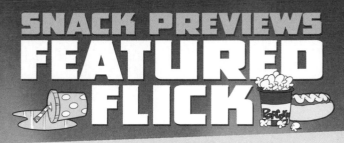

THE GOOD:
Special effects are doggone great!

THE BAD:
Dogs in audience kept booing.

THE SCORE:
(4 paws)

"This movie kicks major canine butt!"

5 paws: A visual slice of heaven · 4 paws: A "reel" treat · 3 paws: Worth a taste · 2 paws: Barely palatable · 1 paw: Gagger

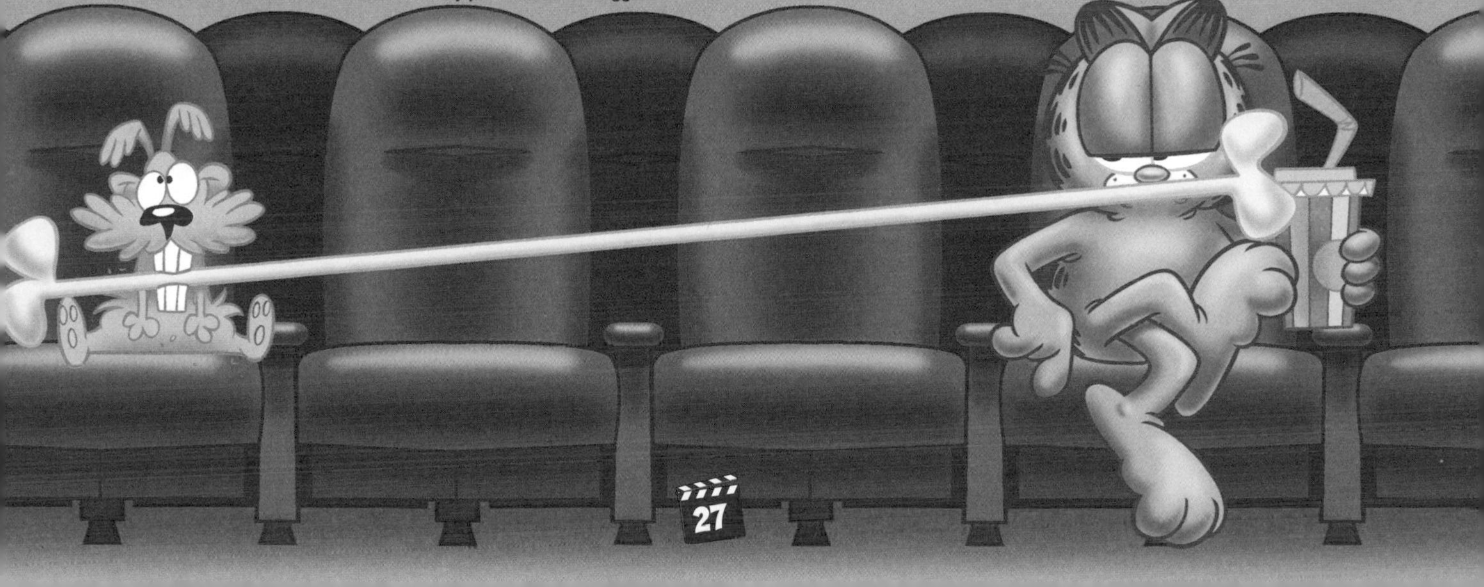

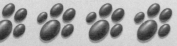

CRIME:

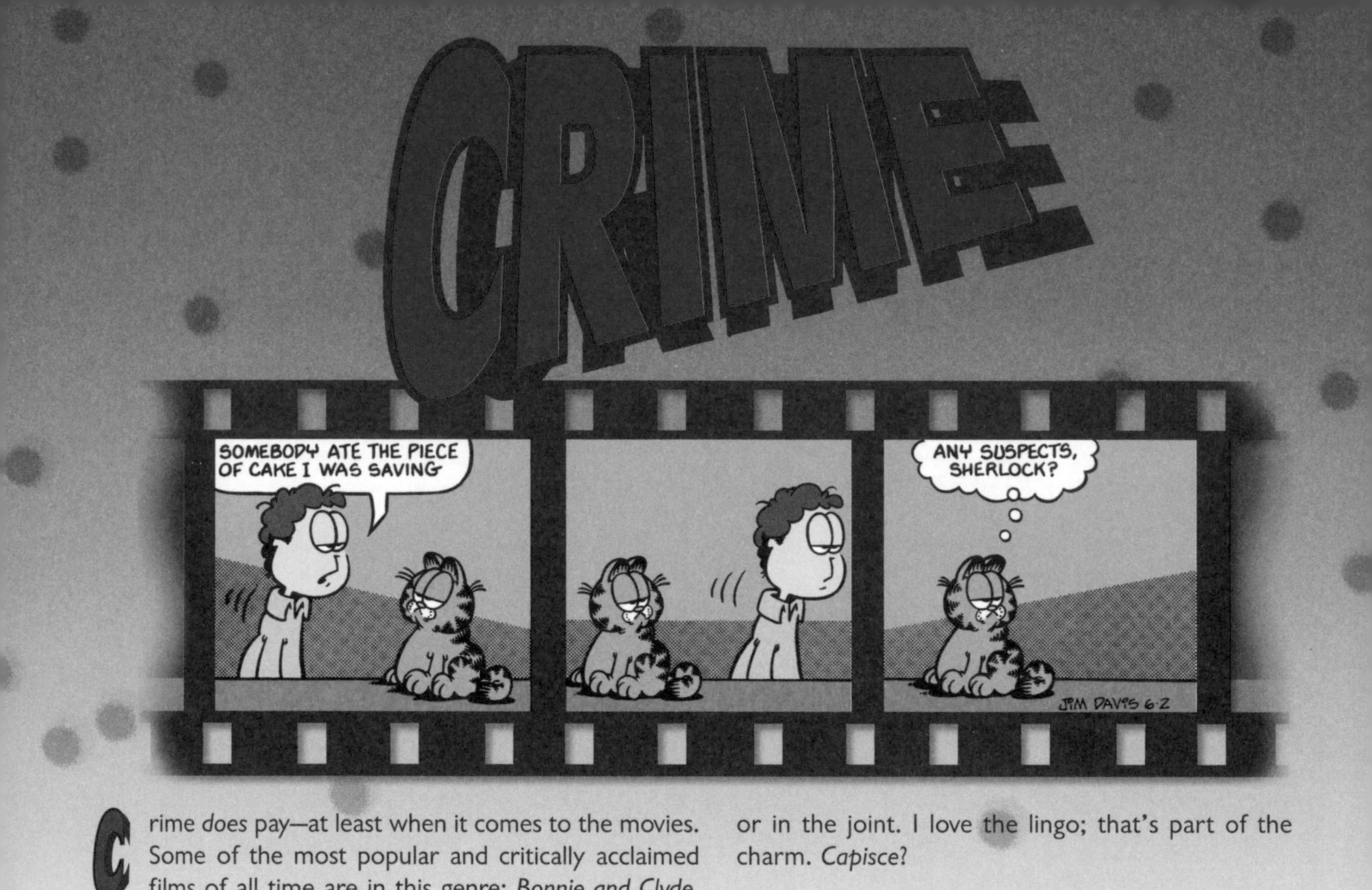
SOMEBODY ATE THE PIECE OF CAKE I WAS SAVING
ANY SUSPECTS, SHERLOCK?
JIM DAVIS 6·2

Crime *does* pay—at least when it comes to the movies. Some of the most popular and critically acclaimed films of all time are in this genre: *Bonnie and Clyde, Chinatown, Pulp Fiction, Goodfellas,* and, of course, *The Godfather*—Parts I and II, that is. Part III should be in cement overshoes, swimming with the fishes!

Gangsters, in particular, seem to fascinate the public, myself included. In fact, I'd make a great mob boss: I'm a wiseguy who's used to giving orders to dumb guys like Jon and Odie. The only thing holding me back is I'm too messy for organized crime. So, instead, I watch movies. I sit on my cushion gawking, while the goombahs and goodfellas go to the mattresses and end up whacked or in the joint. I love the lingo; that's part of the charm. *Capisce*?

Whether people actually admire these robbin' hoods, or just enjoy the vicarious violence is a matter of debate. What's not debatable is that viewers find these films to be wicked fun!

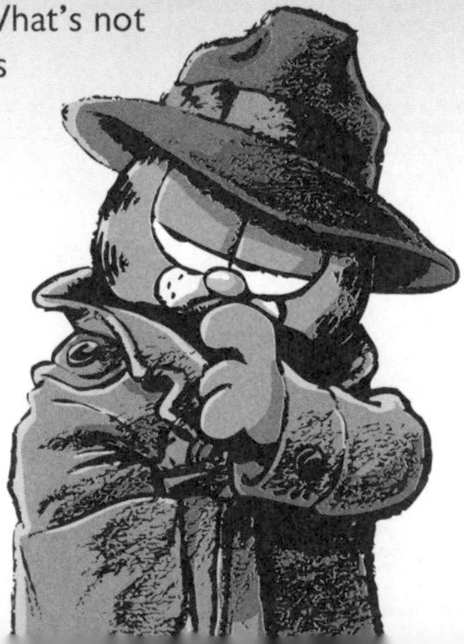

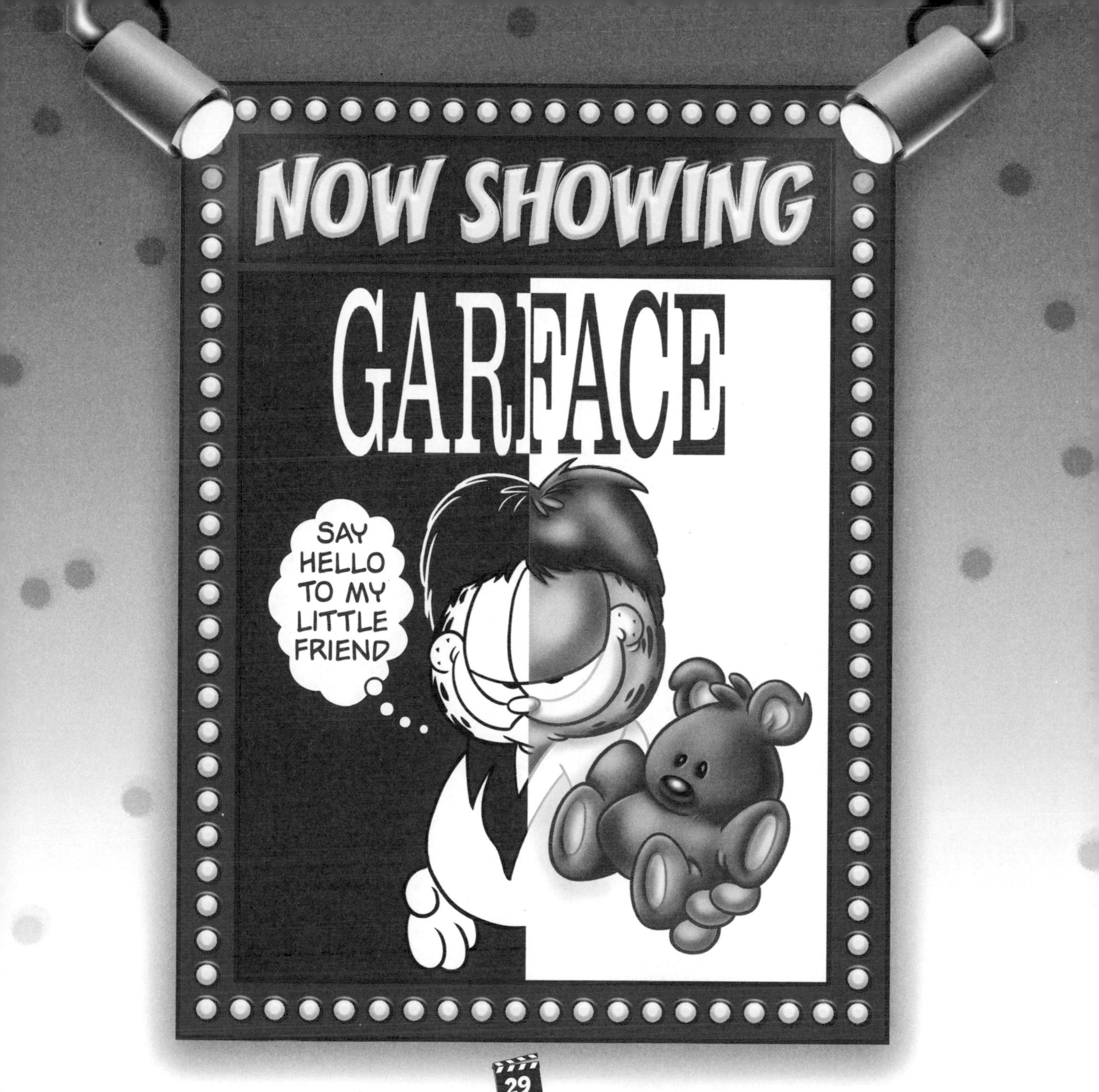
NOW SHOWING
GARFACE
SAY HELLO TO MY LITTLE FRIEND

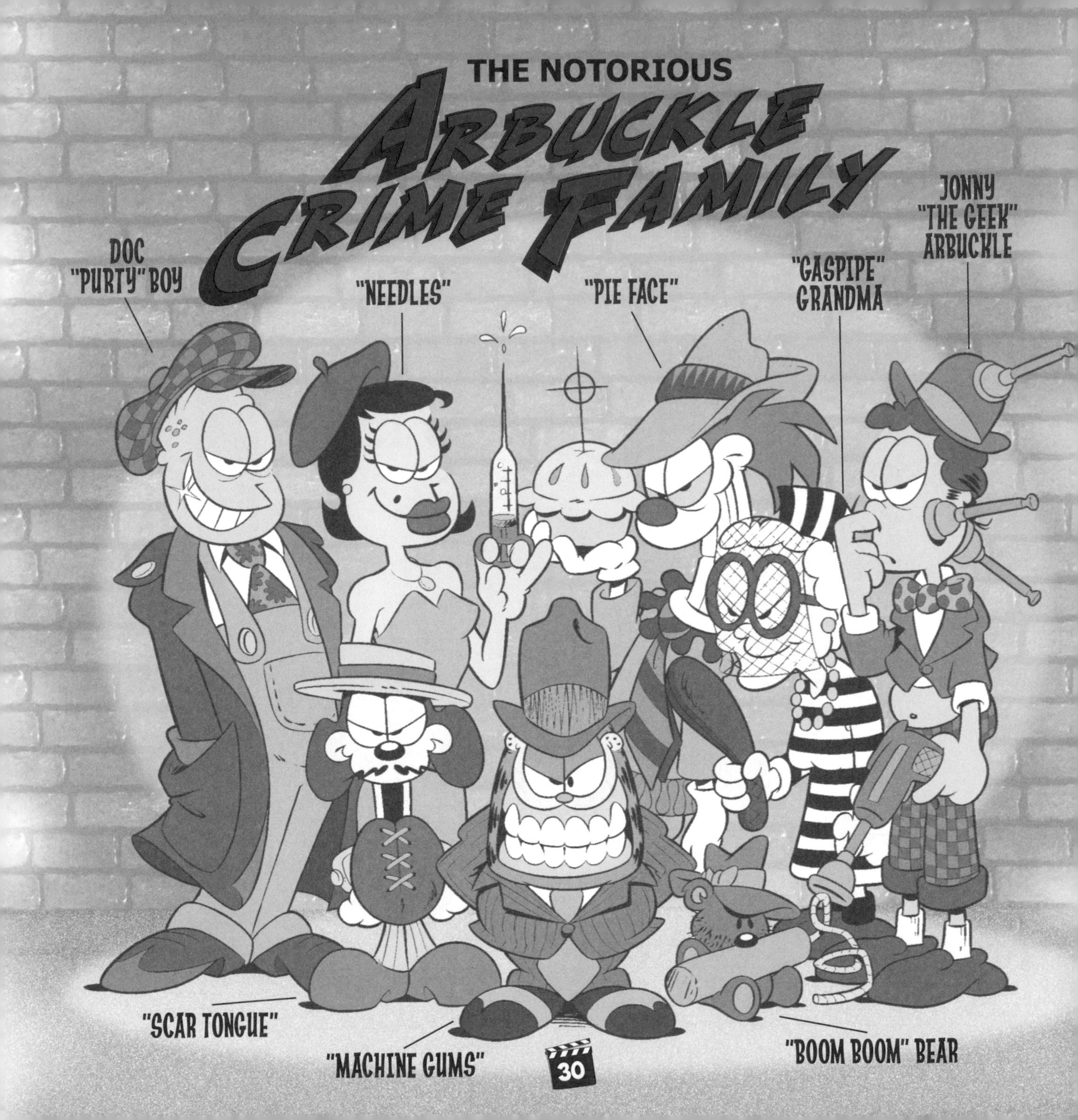
THE NOTORIOUS
ARBUCKLE CRIME FAMILY
DOC "PURTY" BOY
"NEEDLES"
"PIE FACE"
"GASPIPE" GRANDMA
JONNY "THE GEEK" ARBUCKLE
"SCAR TONGUE"
"MACHINE GUMS"
"BOOM BOOM" BEAR

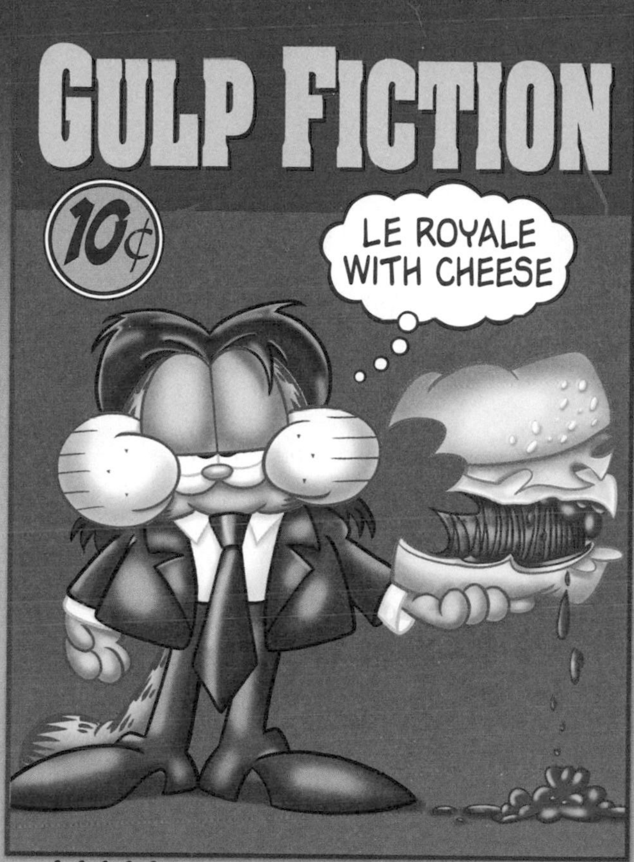
GULP FICTION
10¢
LE ROYALE WITH CHEESE

A visual slice of heaven (5 paws) · A "reel" treat (4 paws) · Worth a taste (3 paws) · Barely palatable (2 paws) · Gagger (1 paw)

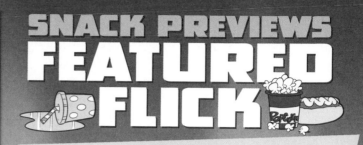

SNACK PREVIEWS FEATURED FLICK

THE GOOD:
A "grooveable" feast for the senses.

THE BAD:
At times, couldn't hear sound track over my growling stomach.

THE SCORE:
(5 paws)

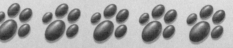

"Take a ride on the wide side! A smorgasbord of killer fun!"

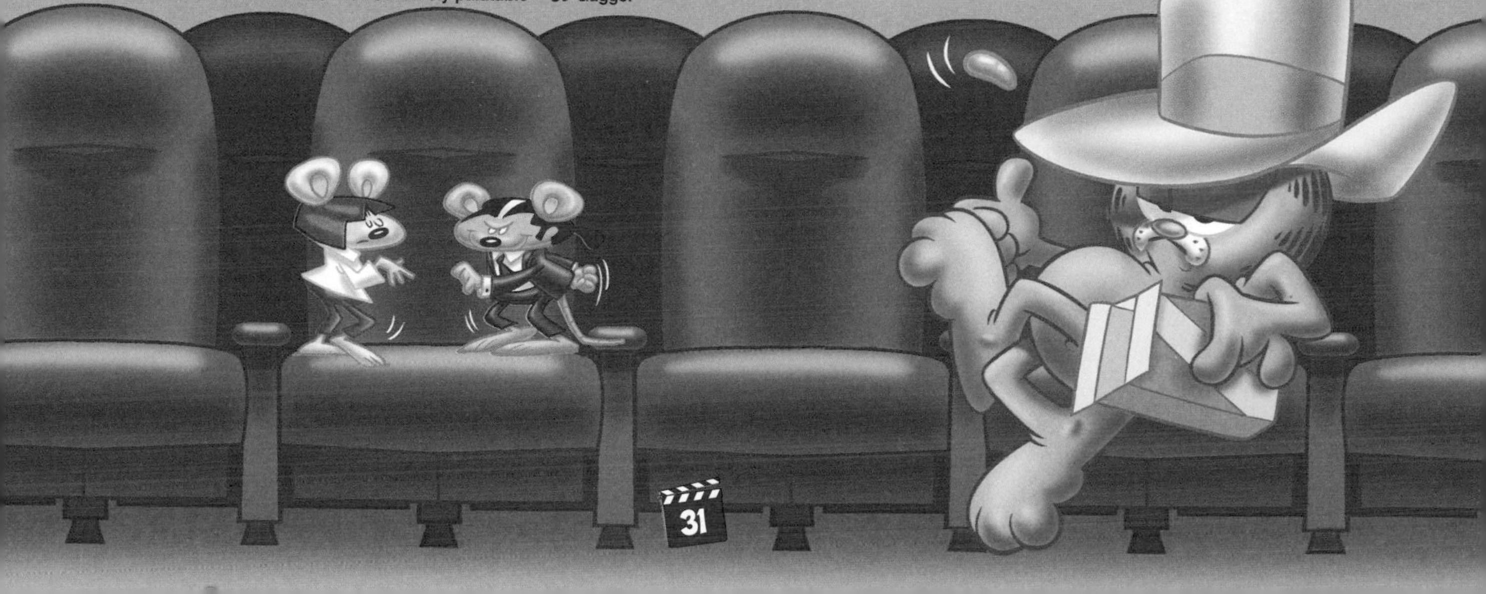

DRAMA

THIS MOVIE LOOKS INTERESTING...

IT'S A COURTROOM DRAMA

I DON'T REALLY GET INTO THOSE

"GODZILLA VS. THE BOARD OF EDUCATION"

HOWEVER...

Dramas are serious stuff. They're big, fat, heavy deals involving intense conflicts and emotions (like when Jon tries to put me on a diet!). The range of conflicts is as wide as my waistline: social, political, racial, marital, medical, legal, criminal, environmental . . . you get the idea.

I particularly like courtroom dramas (*To Kill a Mockingbird*) and prison dramas (*The Shawshank Redemption*). And I'm cuckoo about loony-bin dramas! Actually, they don't even have to take place in a "snake pit," as in *Snake Pit*. I just find it fascinating when movies involve psychiatric conditions, as in *The Three Faces of Eve, Vertigo,* or *A Beautiful Mind*. Who knows, maybe it's all the years I've spent at the Arbuckle asylum with Jon and Odie.

But it's not just me: The critics—and the Academy Award voters—love these movies, too. Dramas are an actor's best friend when it comes to winning awards. A physical disability, a mental illness, or, better yet, a *terminal* illness—preferably while on Death Row—can be a ticket to Oscar® glory. Hey, I'm not cynical; I'm just melodramatic!

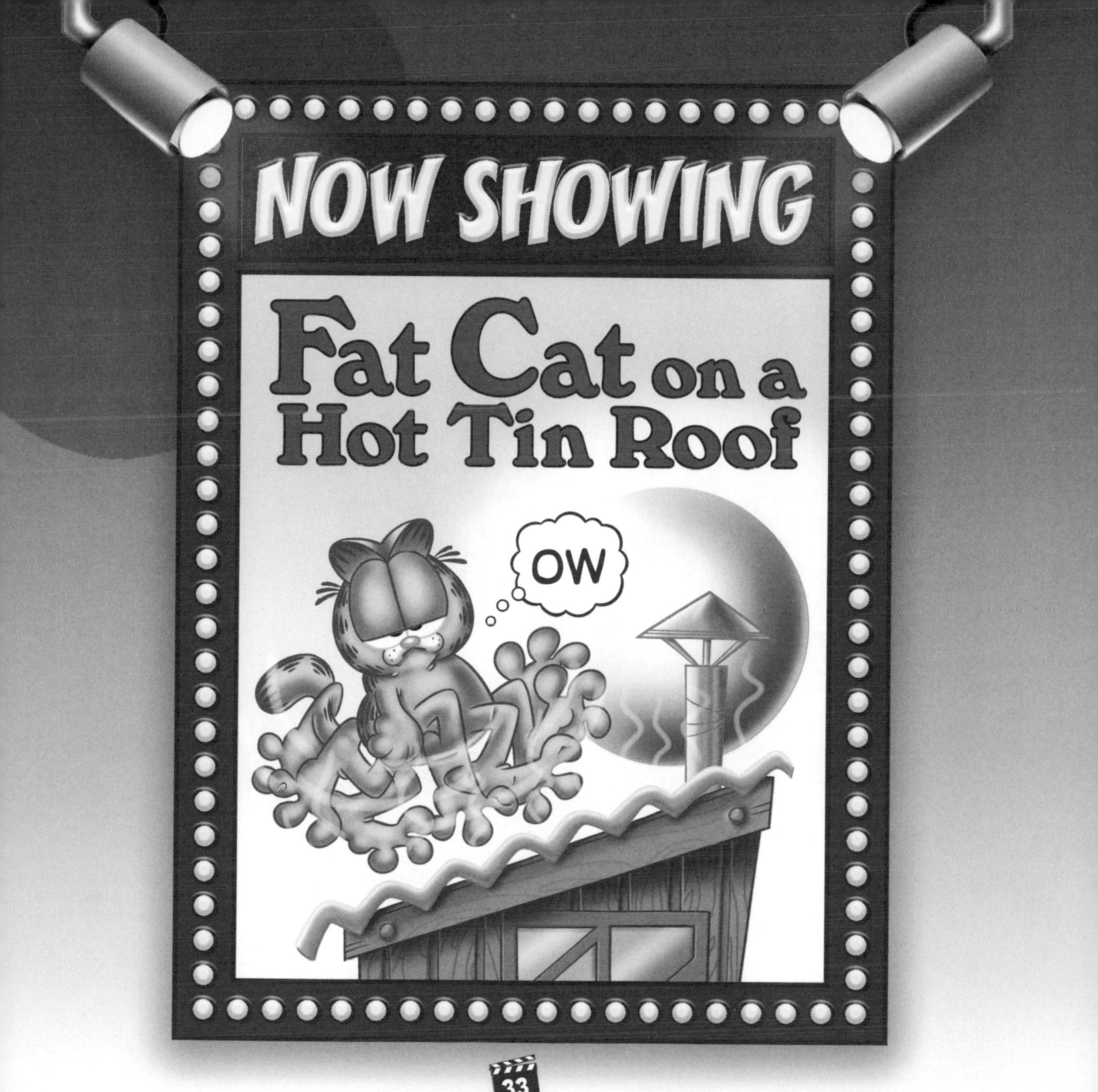
NOW SHOWING
Fat Cat on a Hot Tin Roof
OW

PRINCIPLES OF
METHOD EATING

FEEL

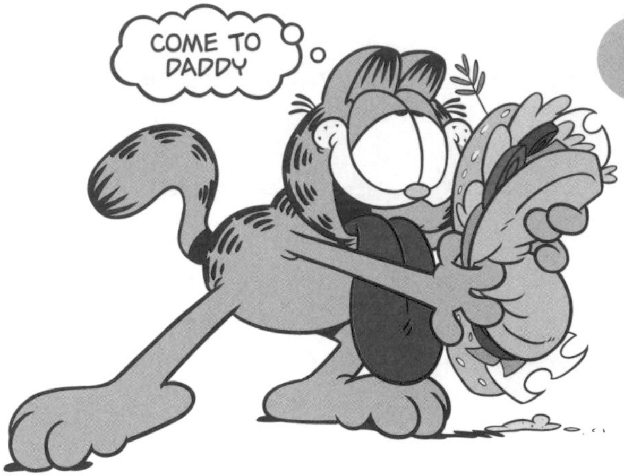
COME TO DADDY

THINK

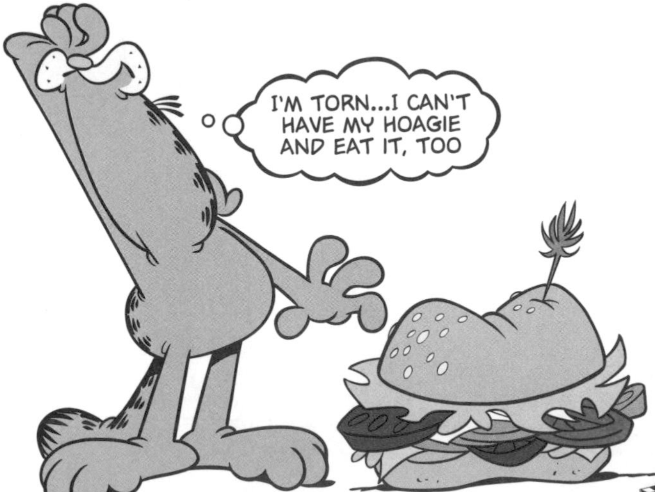
I'M TORN...I CAN'T HAVE MY HOAGIE AND EAT IT, TOO

DO

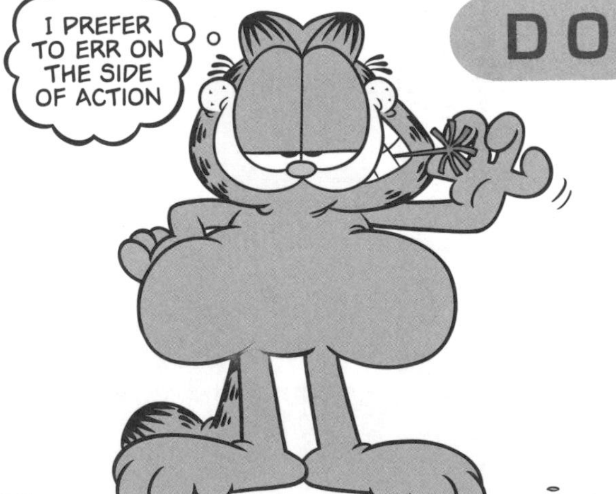
I PREFER TO ERR ON THE SIDE OF ACTION

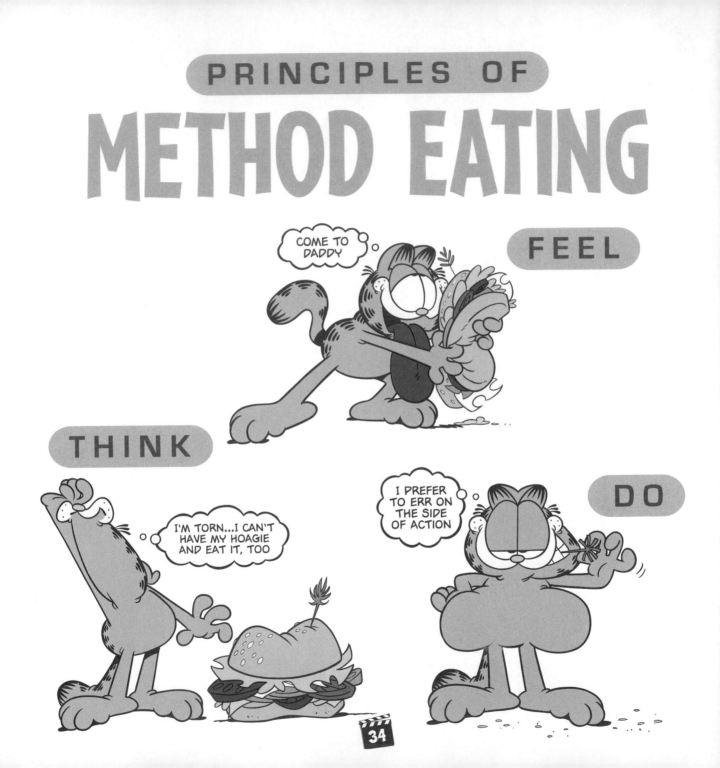

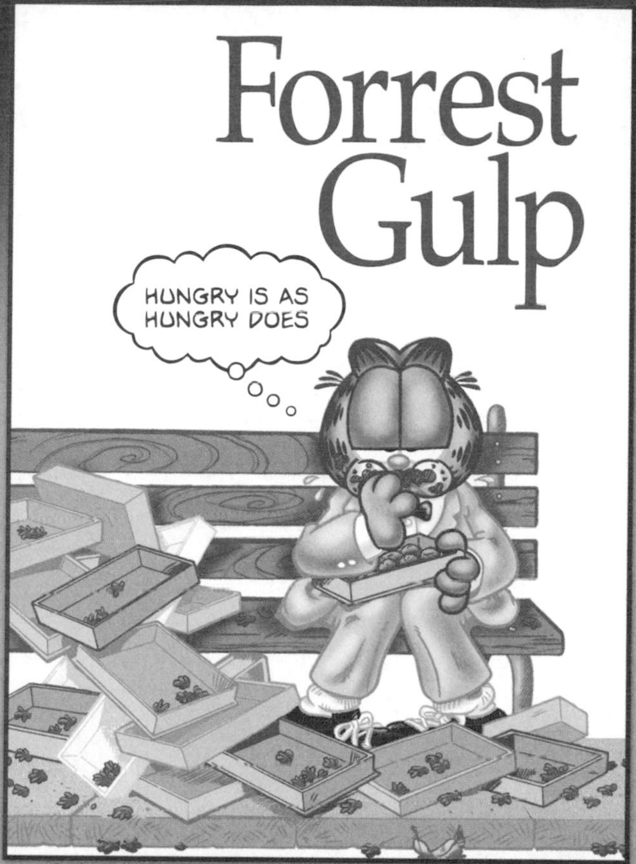
Forrest
Gulp
HUNGRY IS AS HUNGRY DOES

A visual slice of heaven · A "reel" treat · Worth a taste · Barely palatable · Gagger

SNACK PREVIEWS FEATURED FLICK

THE GOOD:

Magical moments with recent historical heavyweights (Elvis, JFK, Nixon...).

THE BAD:

Soppy sweetness could lead to diabetic coma.

THE SCORE:

"This movie is a box of chocolates...dig in and pig out!"

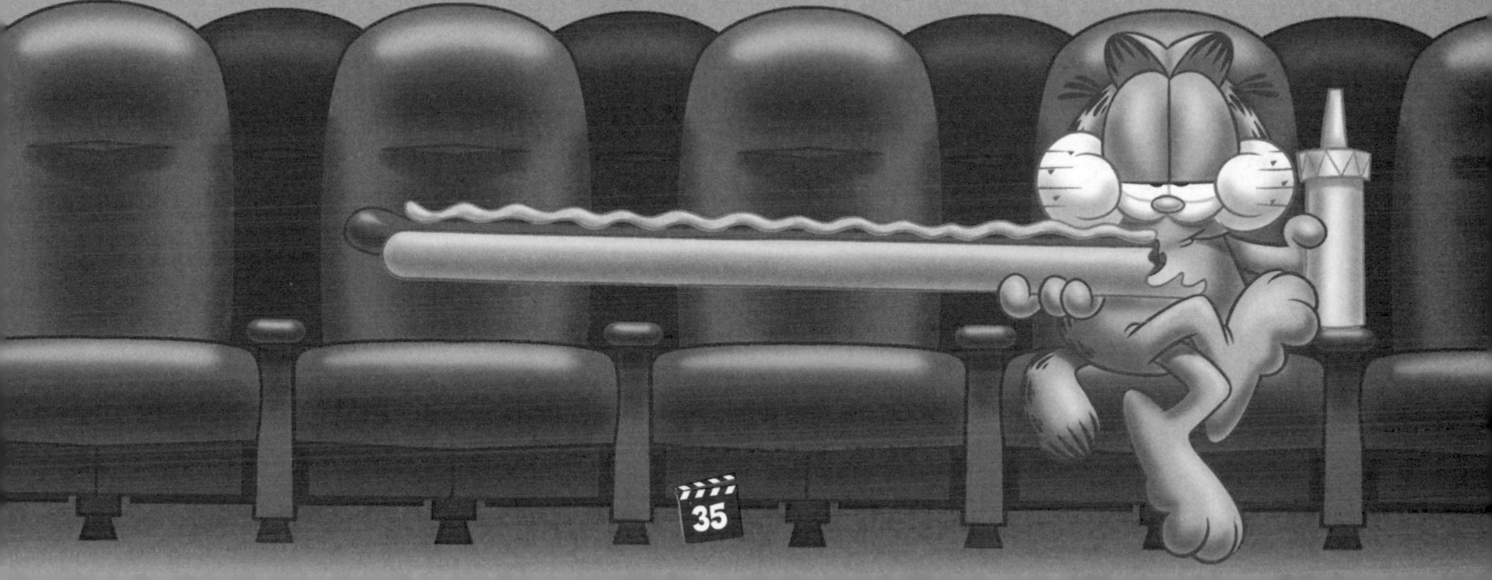

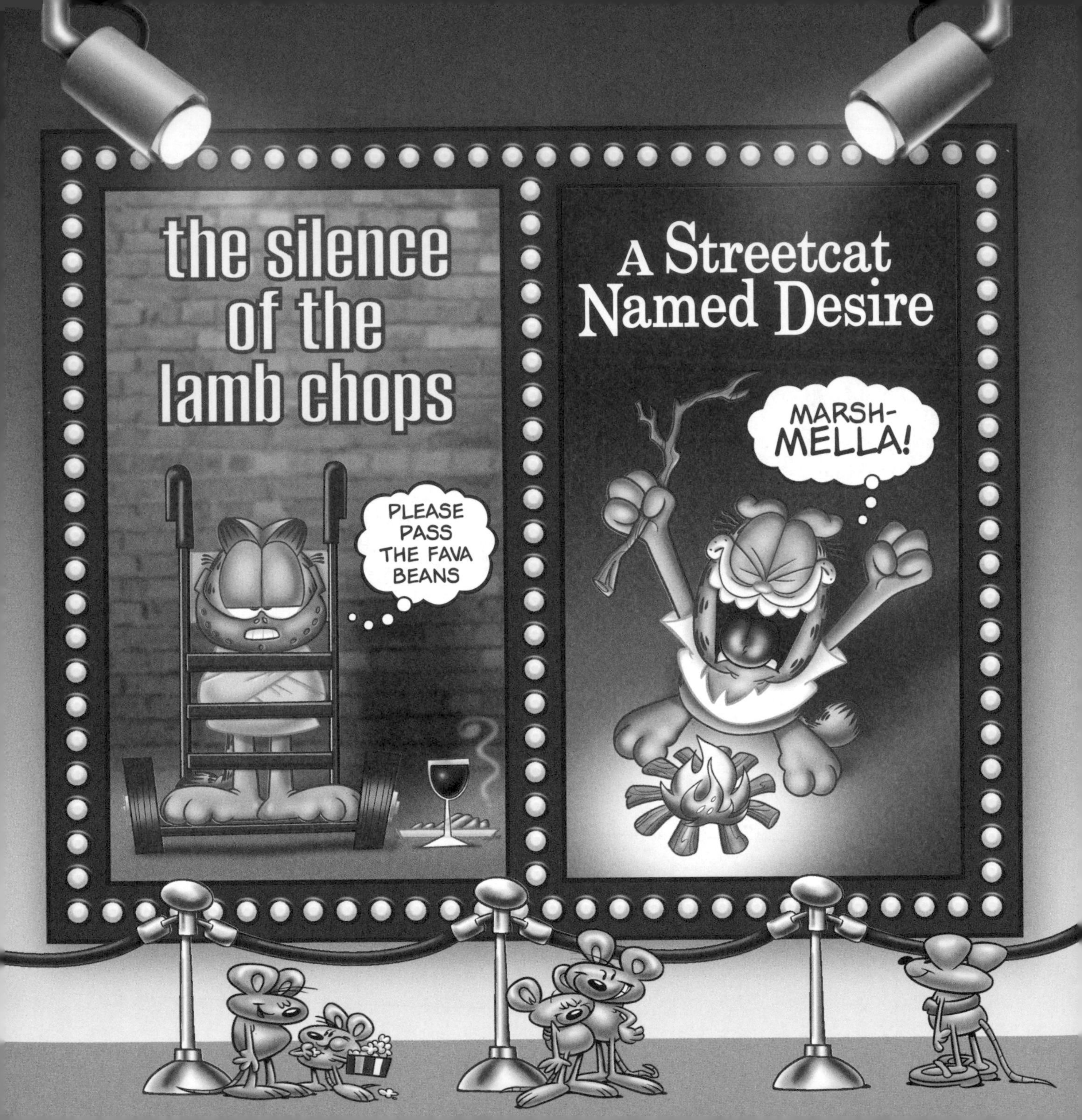

the silence of the lamb chops
PLEASE PASS THE FAVA BEANS
A Streetcat Named Desire
MARSH-MELLA!

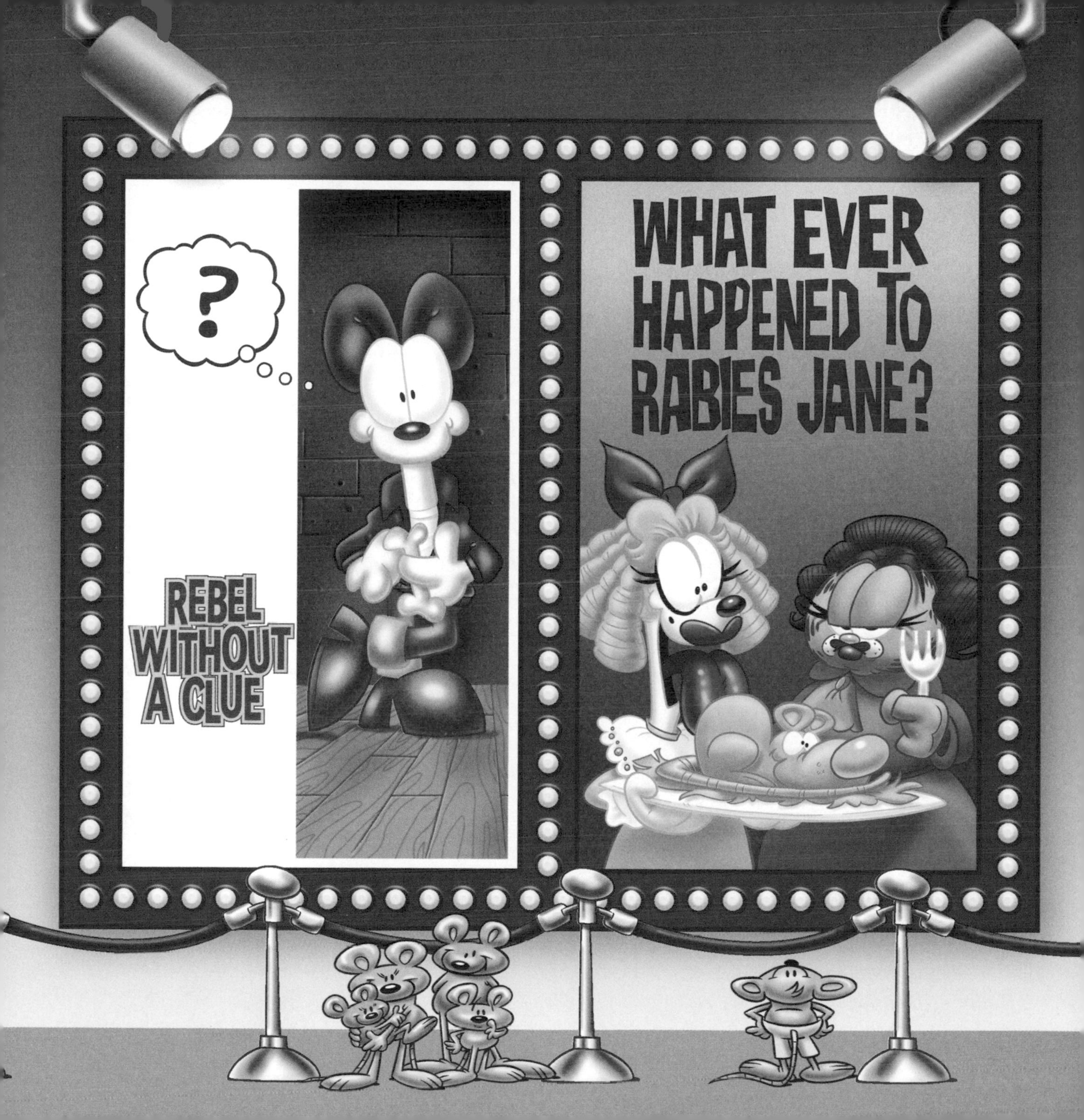
?
REBEL WITHOUT A CLUE
WHAT EVER HAPPENED TO RABIES JANE?

Family

> THE AD SAYS THIS MOVIE IS "FUN FOR THE WHOLE FAMILY"

> HEY, WE'RE FAMILY, RIGHT?

> IN A DYSFUNCTIONAL SORTA WAY

The phrase "fun for the whole family" in a movie ad means different things to different people. To Jon, my ever-dorky owner, it means an enthralling trip to the theater for some good, clean movie-watching; to me it means two hours of slow torture. Don't get me wrong. I'm all for nice bland movies with wholesome messages... as long as I don't have to suffer through them.

When I see the word "heartwarming" used to describe a movie, I know I'm in trouble. I see "heartwarming," I think "sleep-inducing."

But in all fairness, not every family film is a snoozefest. There's *The Wizard of Oz*, *Swiss Family Robinson*, *Tom Sawyer*, and *Willy Wonka & The Chocolate Factory* (sure, the Oompa Loompas are kind of creepy and the songs are annoying, but any flick that features chocolate rivers is on my must-see list!).

And, of course, my all-time favorite family film is *Old Yeller*. I just love a movie with a happy ending.

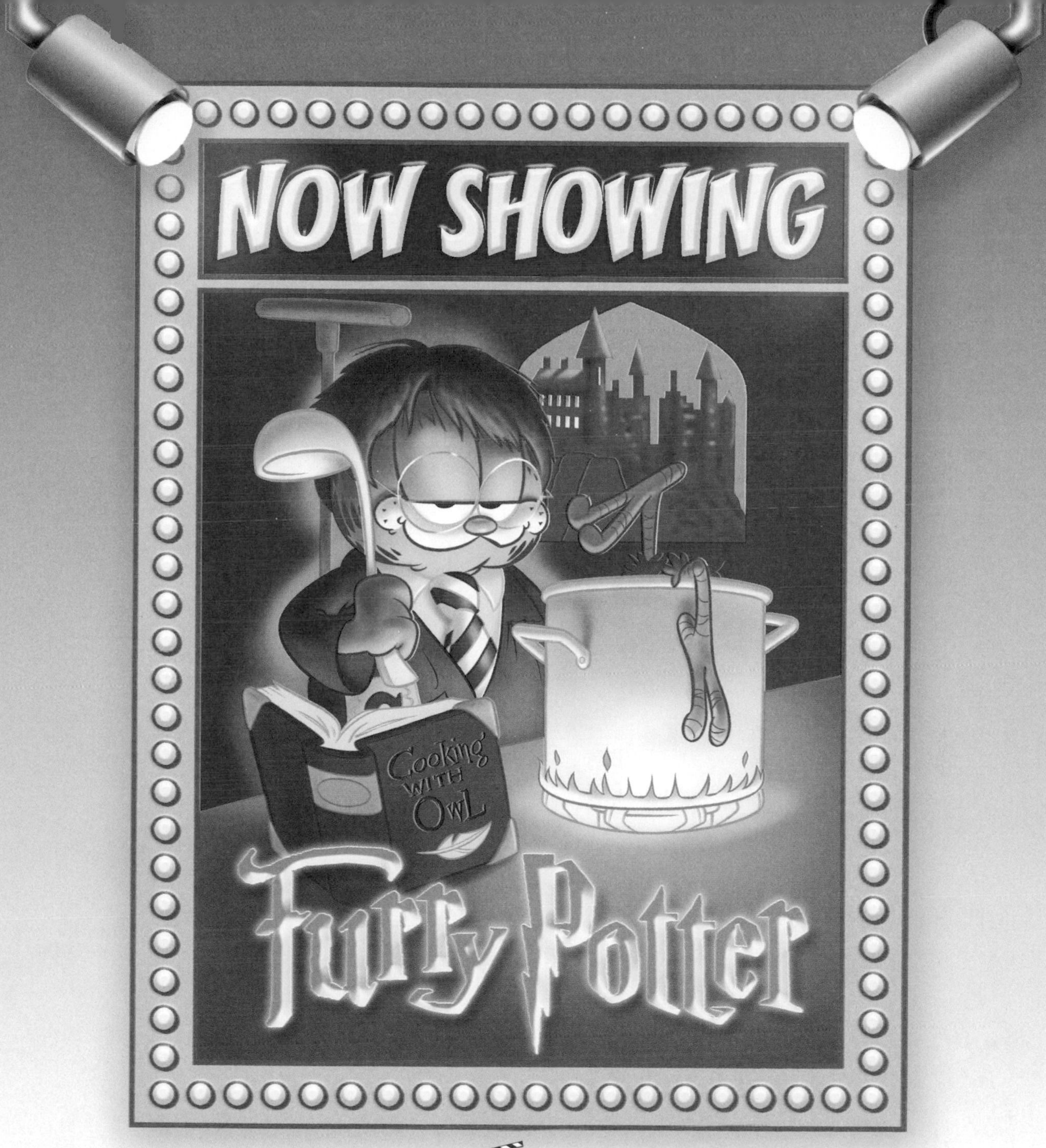
NOW SHOWING
Cooking WITH OWL
Furry Potter

EVEN BIGGER FAMILY-SIZED SNACK BAR TREATS

"YARD-LONG" HOT DOG

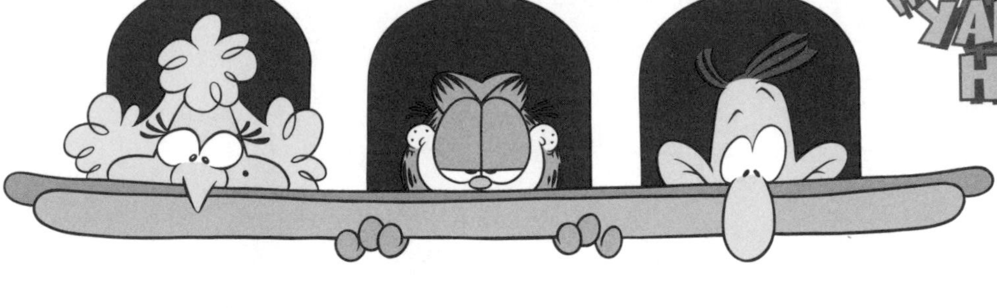

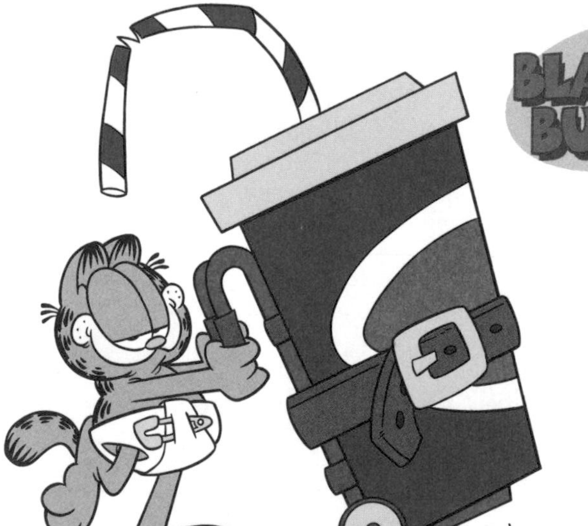

BLADDER BUSTER

SUPER SILO

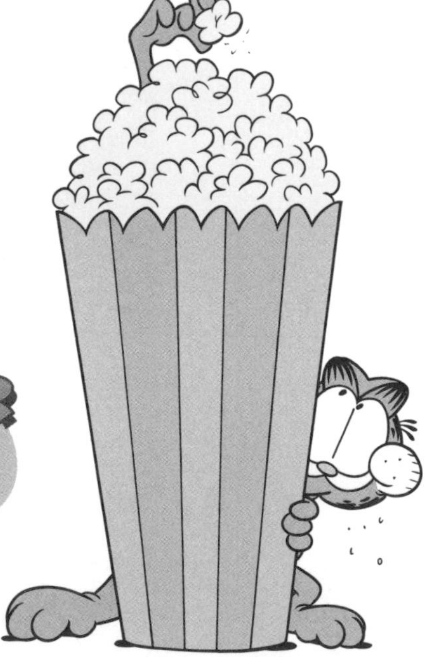

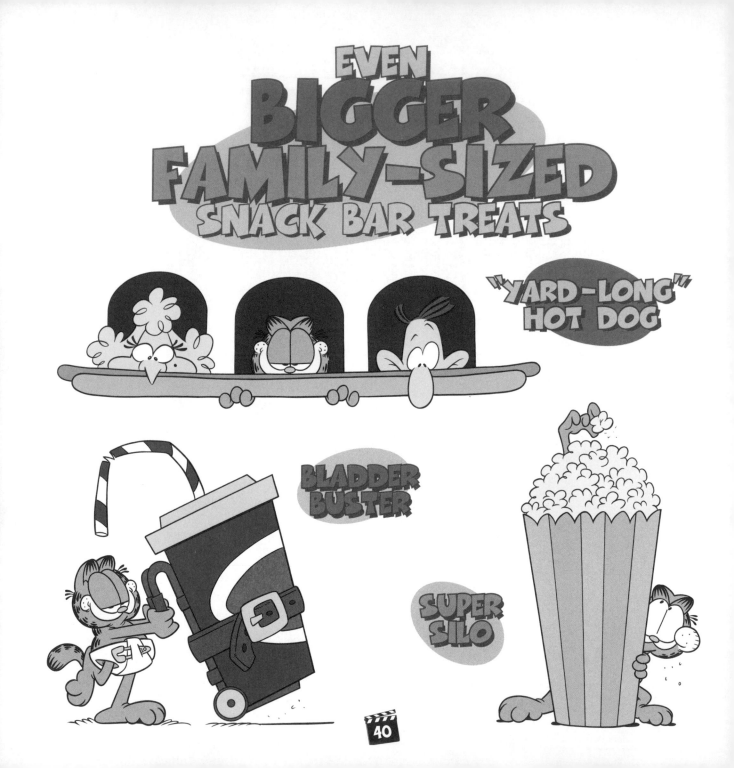

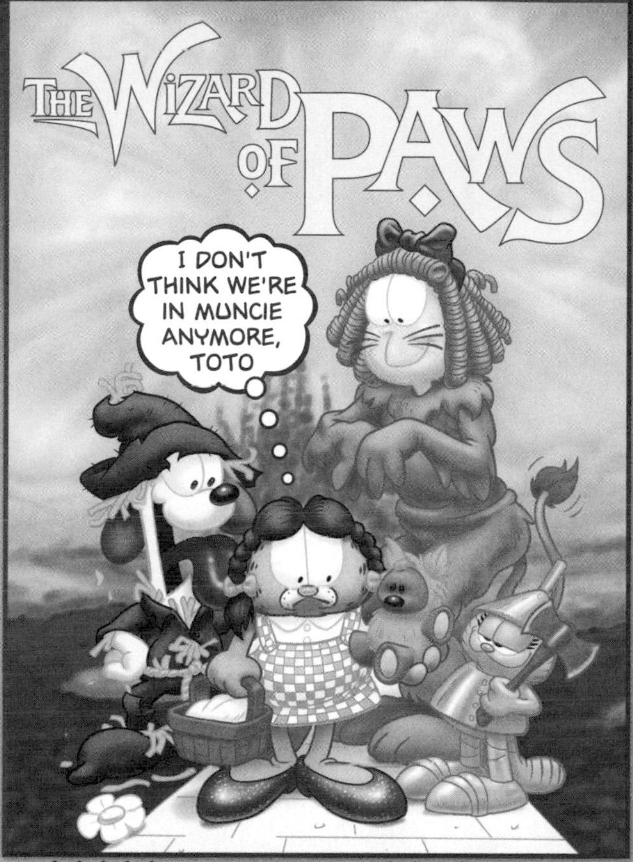
THE WIZARD OF PAWS
I DON'T THINK WE'RE IN MUNCIE ANYMORE, TOTO

A visual slice of heaven · A "reel" treat · Worth a taste · Barely palatable · Gagger

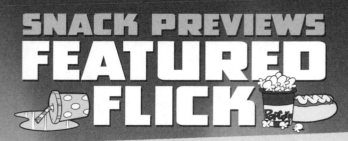

SNACK PREVIEWS FEATURED FLICK

THE GOOD:

Everything! There's no place like home…and there's no movie like this!

THE BAD:

What? Criticize this picture and I'll get you—and your little dog, too!

THE SCORE:

"You'd have to go somewhere over the rainbow to find a finer film."

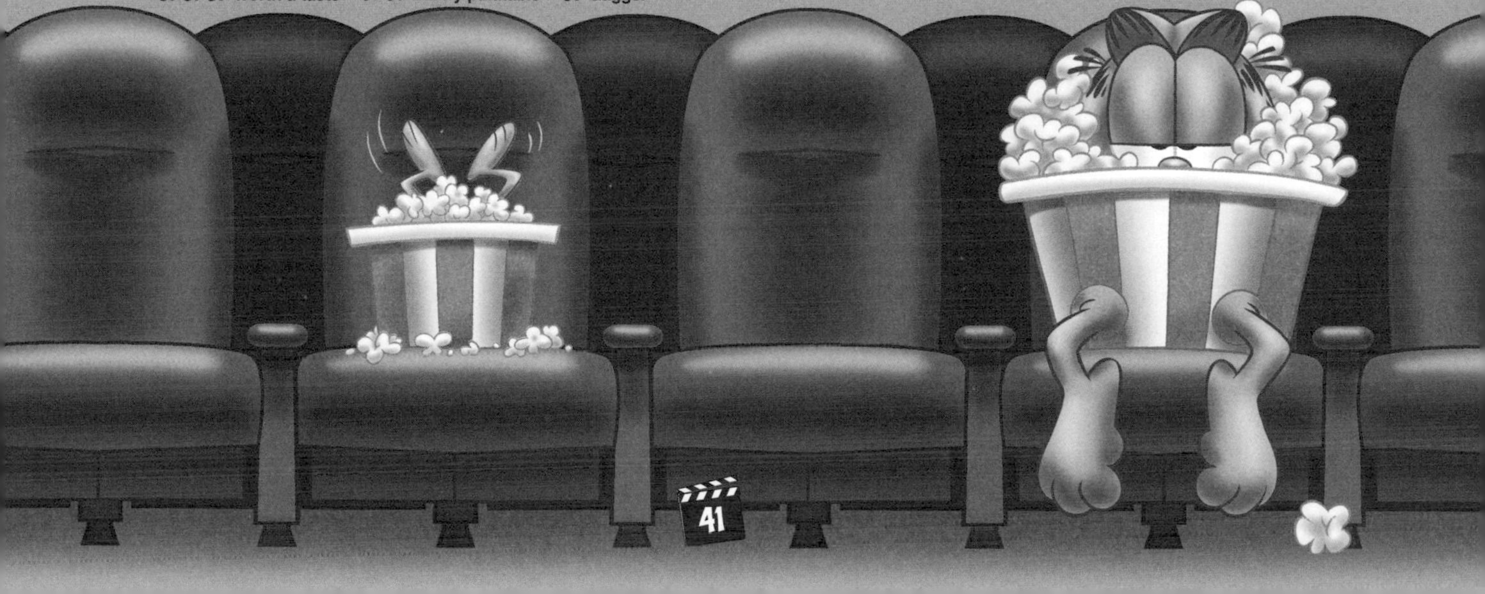

HISTORICAL EPICS

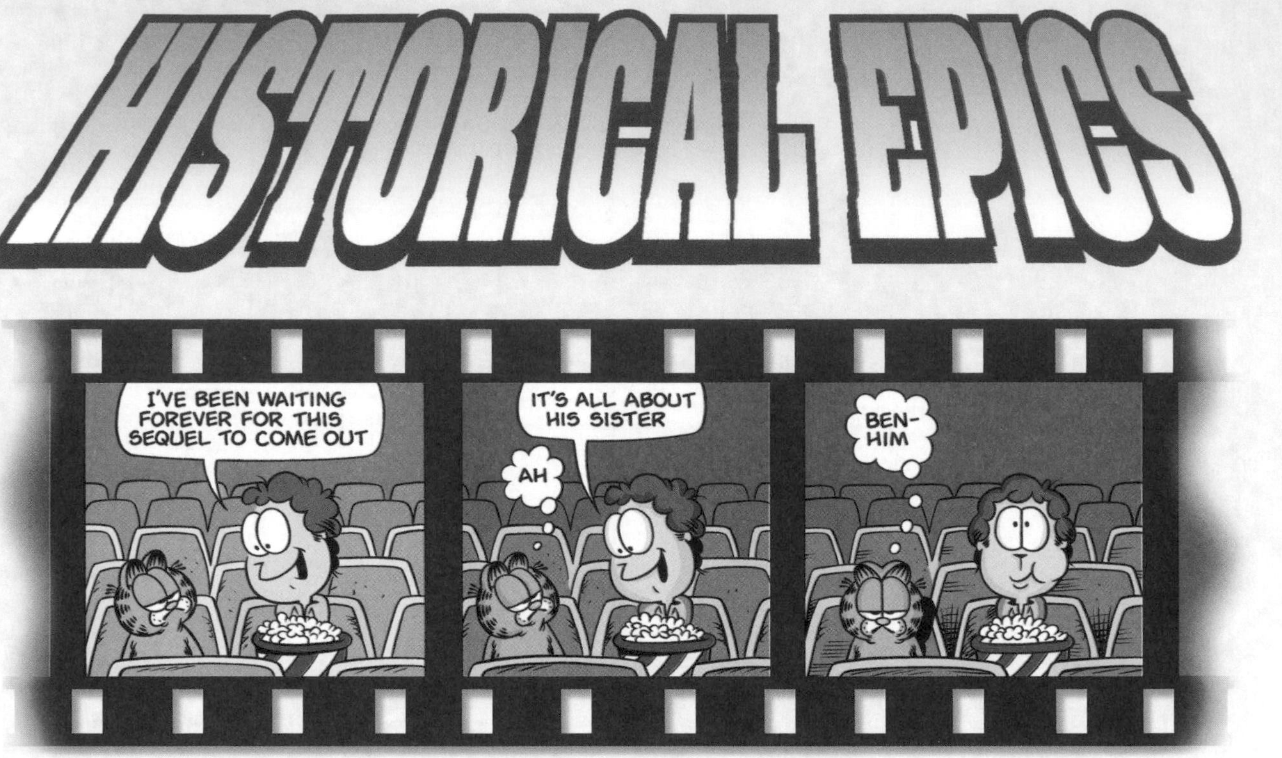

I'VE BEEN WAITING FOREVER FOR THIS SEQUEL TO COME OUT
IT'S ALL ABOUT HIS SISTER
AH
BEN-HIM

Epics are big, proud, Texas-size movies. They sprawl across the screen on a grand scale with grand themes, recounting the deeds of legendary or historical figures. I tend to like the "sword 'n' sandals" sagas such as *Ben-Hur* (with its famous chariot scene—giddyup!) and *Spartacus*. But then, *Alexander* was far from great, and *Troy* was Greek to me. *Lawrence of Arabia* is generally regarded as being at the head of this history class.

These lavish films often have casts of thousands and costs of millions. Actually, that can be more like *hundreds* of millions now. These days *The Ten Commandments* would carry a price tag of biblical proportions. Thou shalt not make epics on the cheap.

I hold epics in high esteem, but I don't always enjoy them. They feature cool costumes, exotic locations, and often spectacular action. But the number-one characteristic of these king-size flicks is that they're loooong. And that can be a royal pain for those of us with short attention spans, small bladders, and growling stomachs. So, while these epics are better on the big screen (aren't all movies?), I sometimes wait for the DVD to do my three-hour tour; that way, I can pause for the cause.

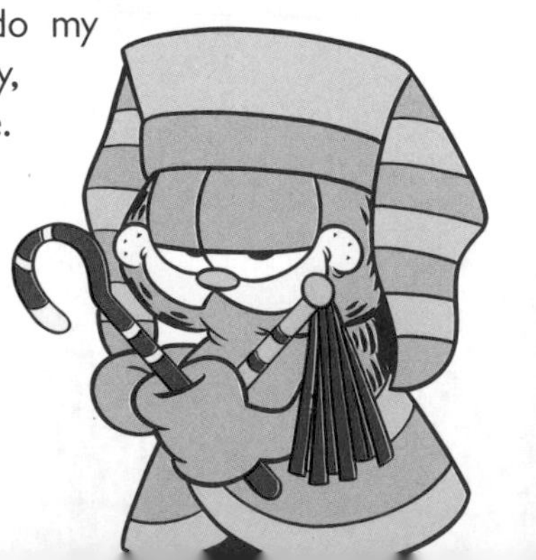

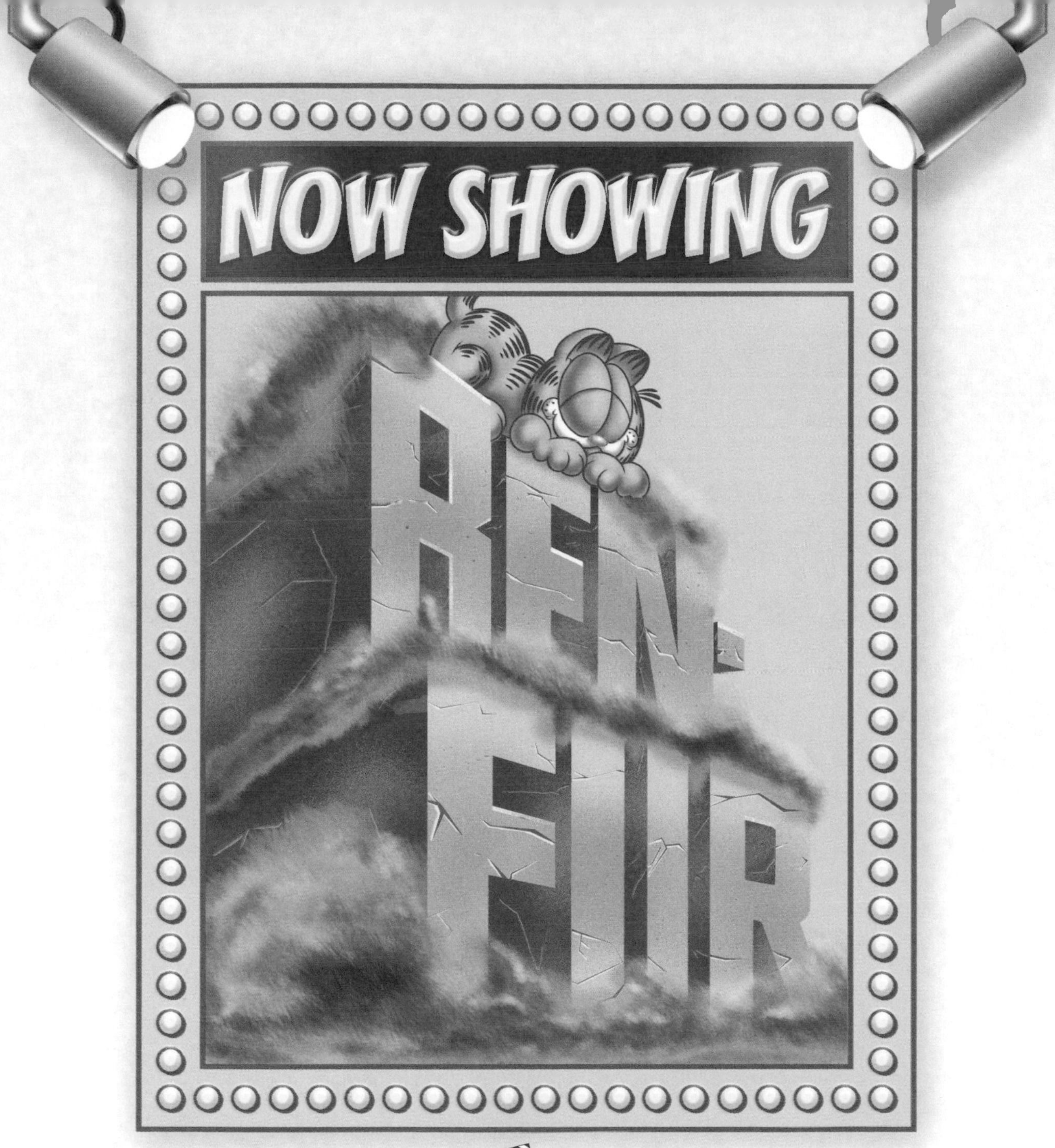
NOW SHOWING
BEN-FUR

HORROR

Panel 1: TONIGHT, A MAD SCIENTIST PUTS A DOG'S BRAIN INTO A ZOMBIE

Panel 2: IN THE HORROR CLASSIC...

Panel 3: "NIGHT OF THE LIVING DUMB" — WHAT A CRUEL THING TO DO TO A ZOMBIE

Who doesn't like a good scary movie? Even a bad scary movie can be good! (In fact, some of the low-budget horror movies of the 1950s almost qualify as comedies.)

Film fans have yearned to be frightened since the very beginning of movies. One of Thomas Edison's first forays into moving pictures was a 15-minute version of *Frankenstein* in 1910 (alas, the monster looked less like Boris Karloff and more like Bozo the Clown).

It's hard to believe today, but the horror movies of the 1930s actually terrified moviegoers. Now it takes sixty gallons of fake blood and $120 million of CG effects to do the job.

I've always loved watching horror movies. Classic Universal monsters, garish Hammer remakes, Roger Corman's cheesy flicks, even a few of the slasher films. It's all good, gruesome fun. The only film that ever really bothered me was *The Exorcist*. I had a devil of a time sitting through that one. Plus it made me never want to eat pea soup again.

If I was gonna be a horror character, I'd pick Dracula. He sleeps all day and eats all night. My kind of monster! Jon would be Dorkenstein and Odie would be a brainless zombie. Come to think of it, Odie already *is* a brainless zombie.

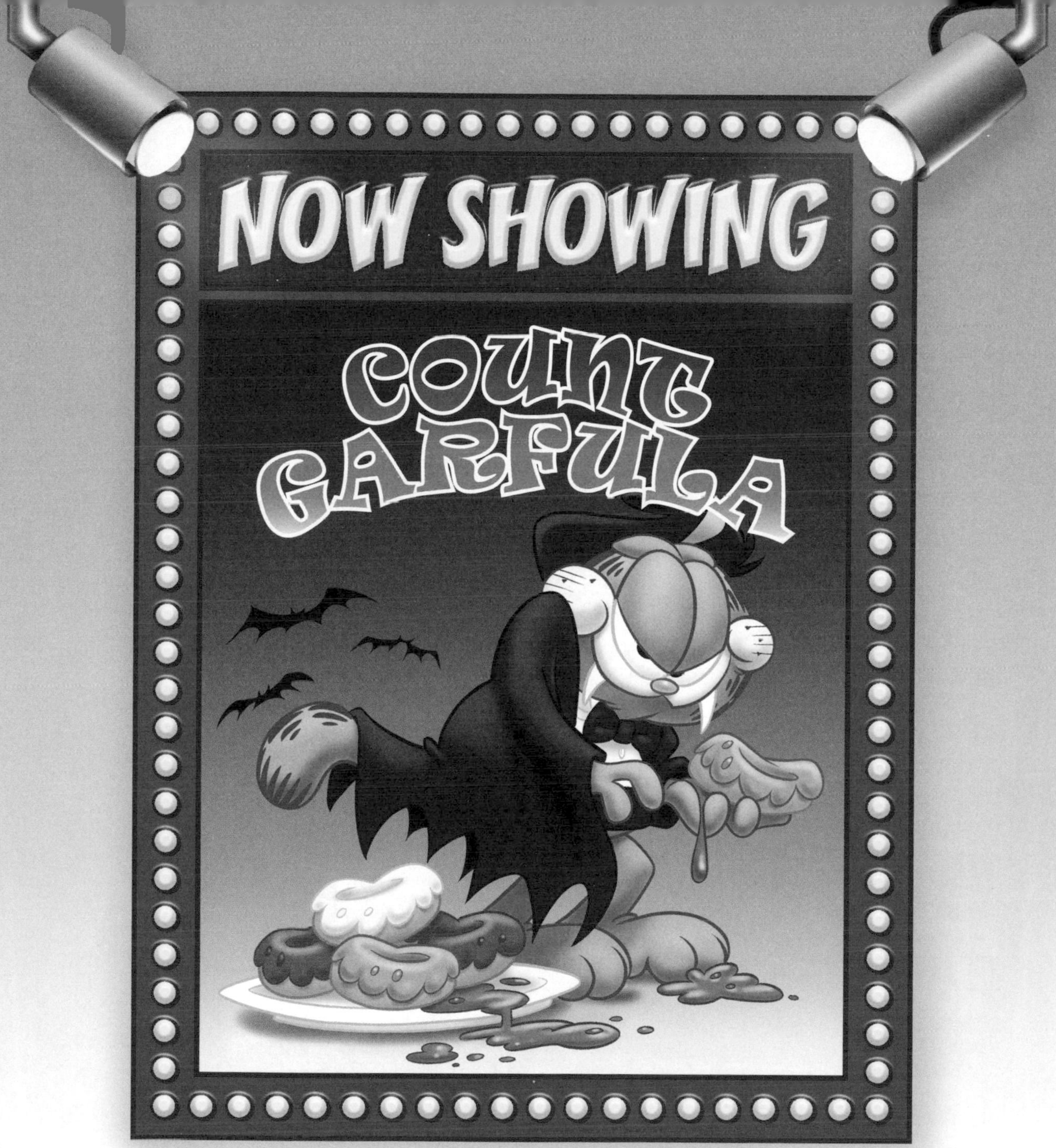
NOW SHOWING
COUNT GARFULA

FOOD FRIGHT

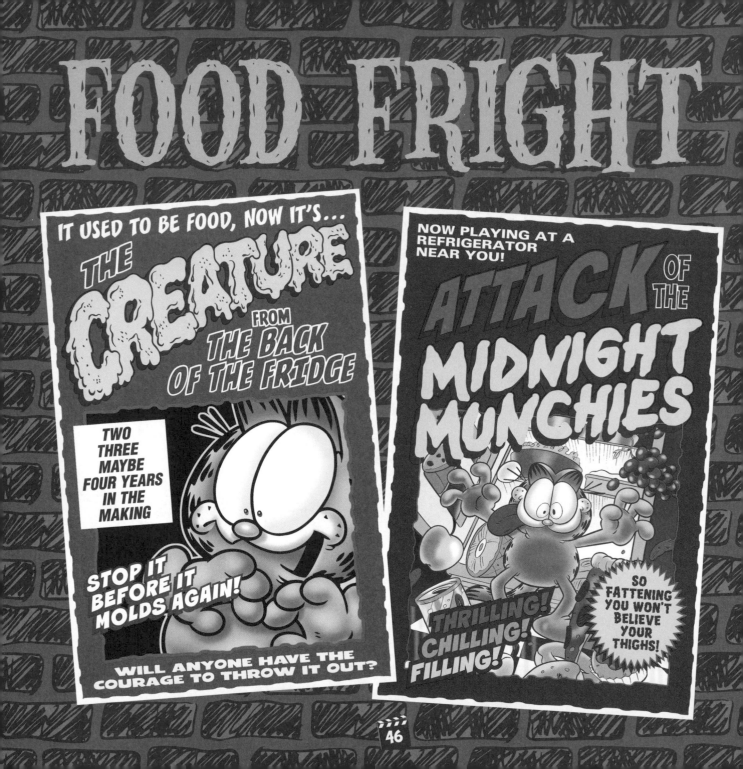

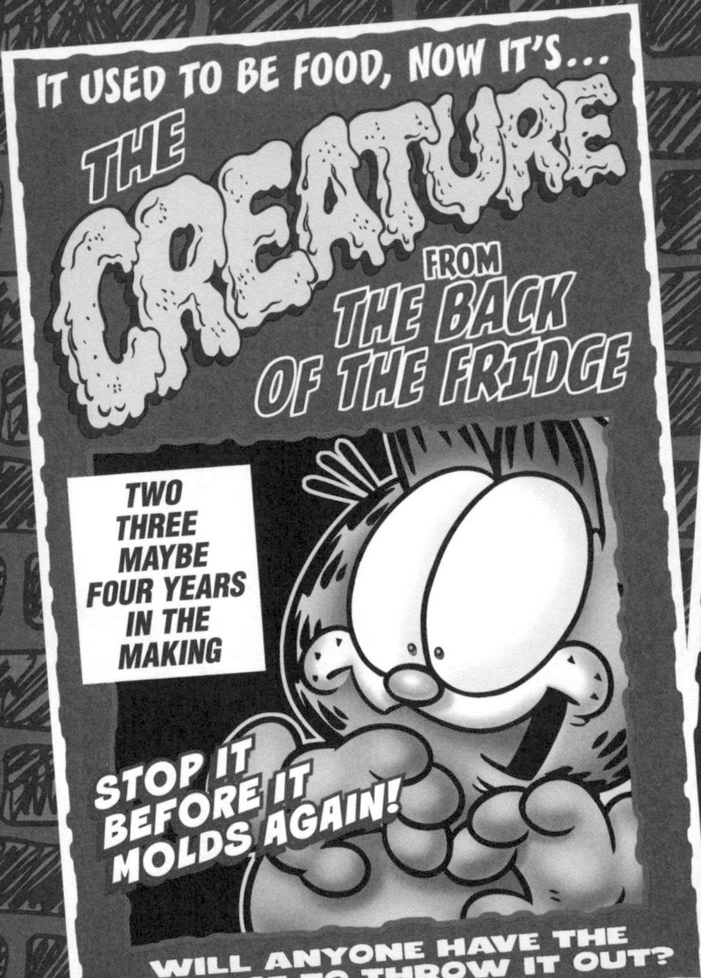
IT USED TO BE FOOD, NOW IT'S...
THE CREATURE FROM THE BACK OF THE FRIDGE
TWO THREE MAYBE FOUR YEARS IN THE MAKING
STOP IT BEFORE IT MOLDS AGAIN!
WILL ANYONE HAVE THE COURAGE TO THROW IT OUT?

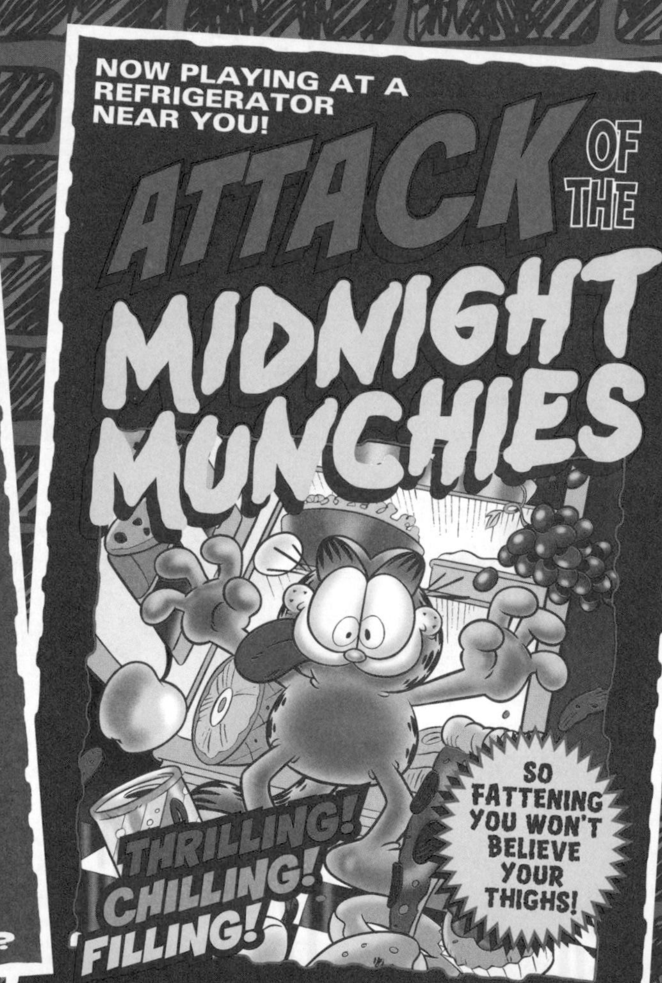
NOW PLAYING AT A REFRIGERATOR NEAR YOU!
ATTACK OF THE MIDNIGHT MUNCHIES
THRILLING! CHILLING! FILLING!
SO FATTENING YOU WON'T BELIEVE YOUR THIGHS!

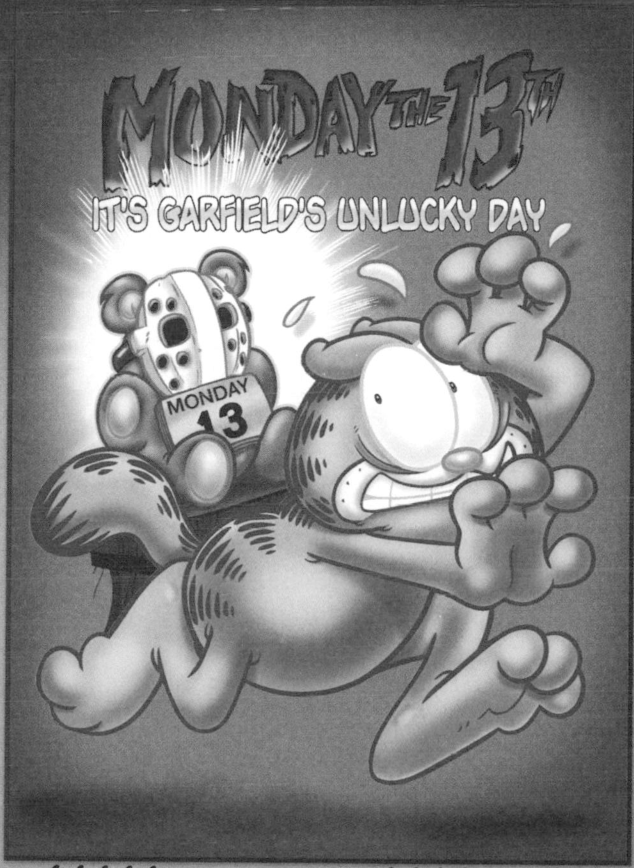
MONDAY THE 13TH
IT'S GARFIELD'S UNLUCKY DAY
MONDAY
13

SNACK PREVIEWS FEATURED FLICK

THE GOOD:
This slasher movie is a cut above the competition.

THE BAD:
Onscreen bloodshed gets pretty draining.

THE SCORE:
(2 paws)

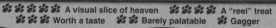

"Almost as scary as a real Monday!"

(5 paws) A visual slice of heaven (4 paws) A "reel" treat
(3 paws) Worth a taste (2 paws) Barely palatable (1 paw) Gagger

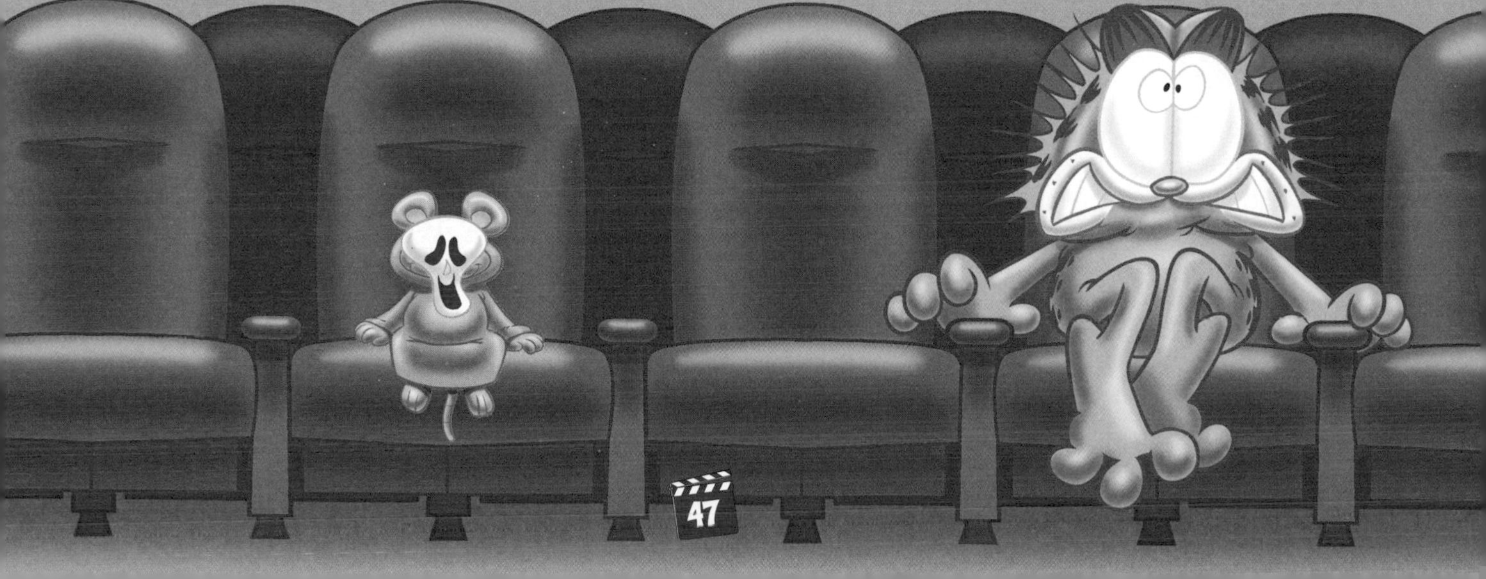

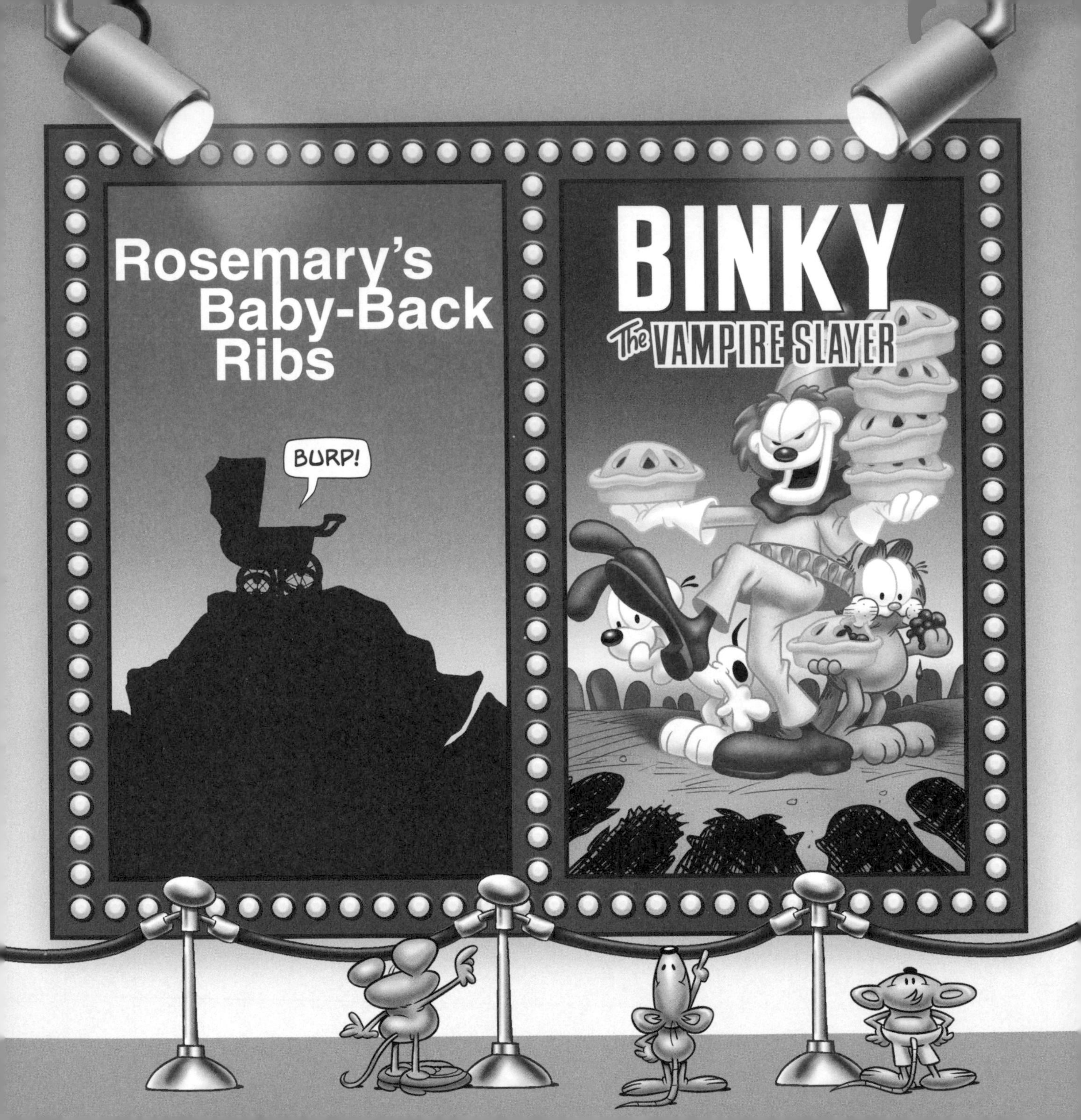
Rosemary's Baby-Back Ribs
BURP!
BINKY
The VAMPIRE SLAYER

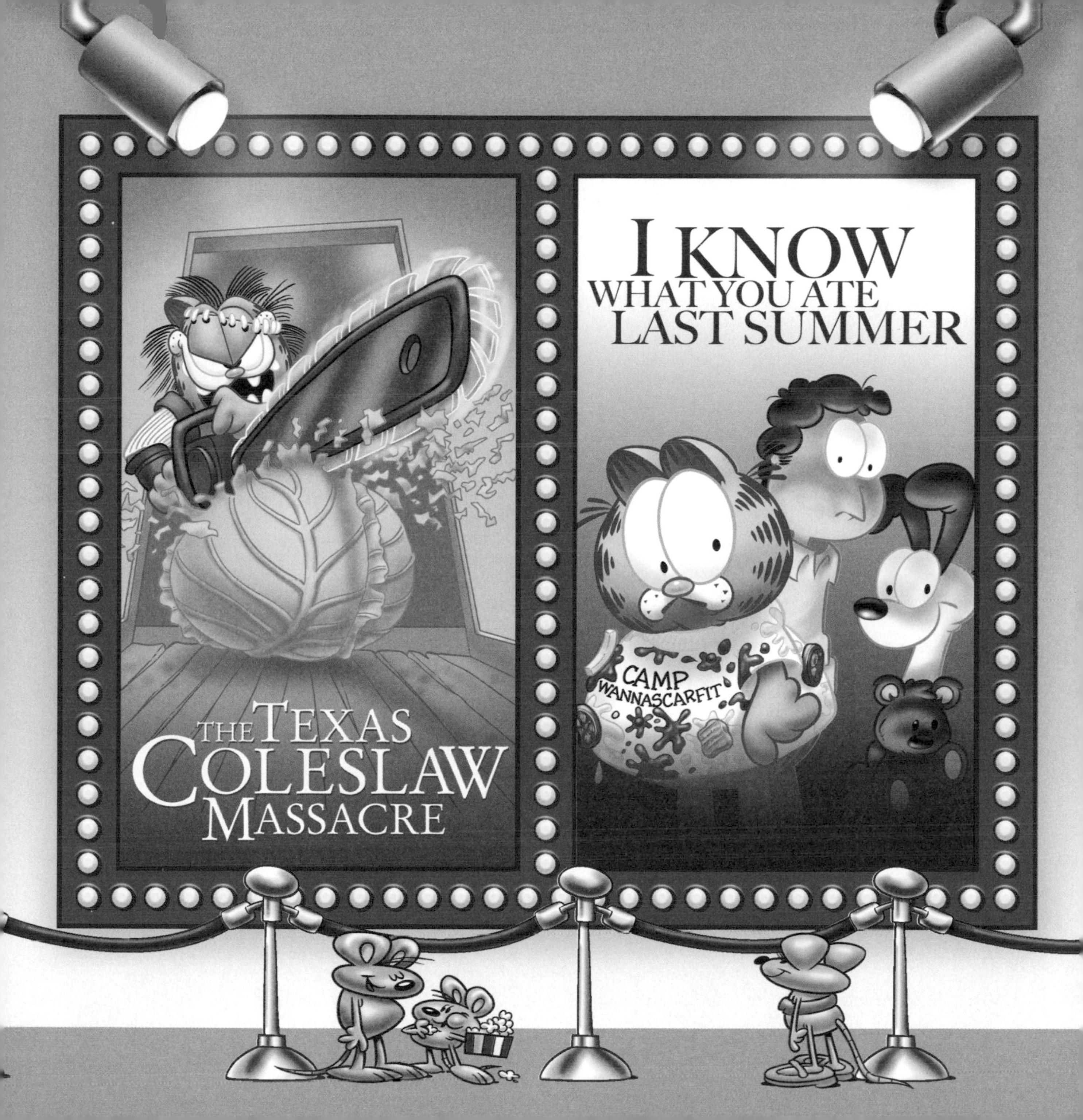
THE TEXAS
COLESLAW
MASSACRE
I KNOW
WHAT YOU ATE
LAST SUMMER
CAMP
WANNASCARFIT

MUSICALS

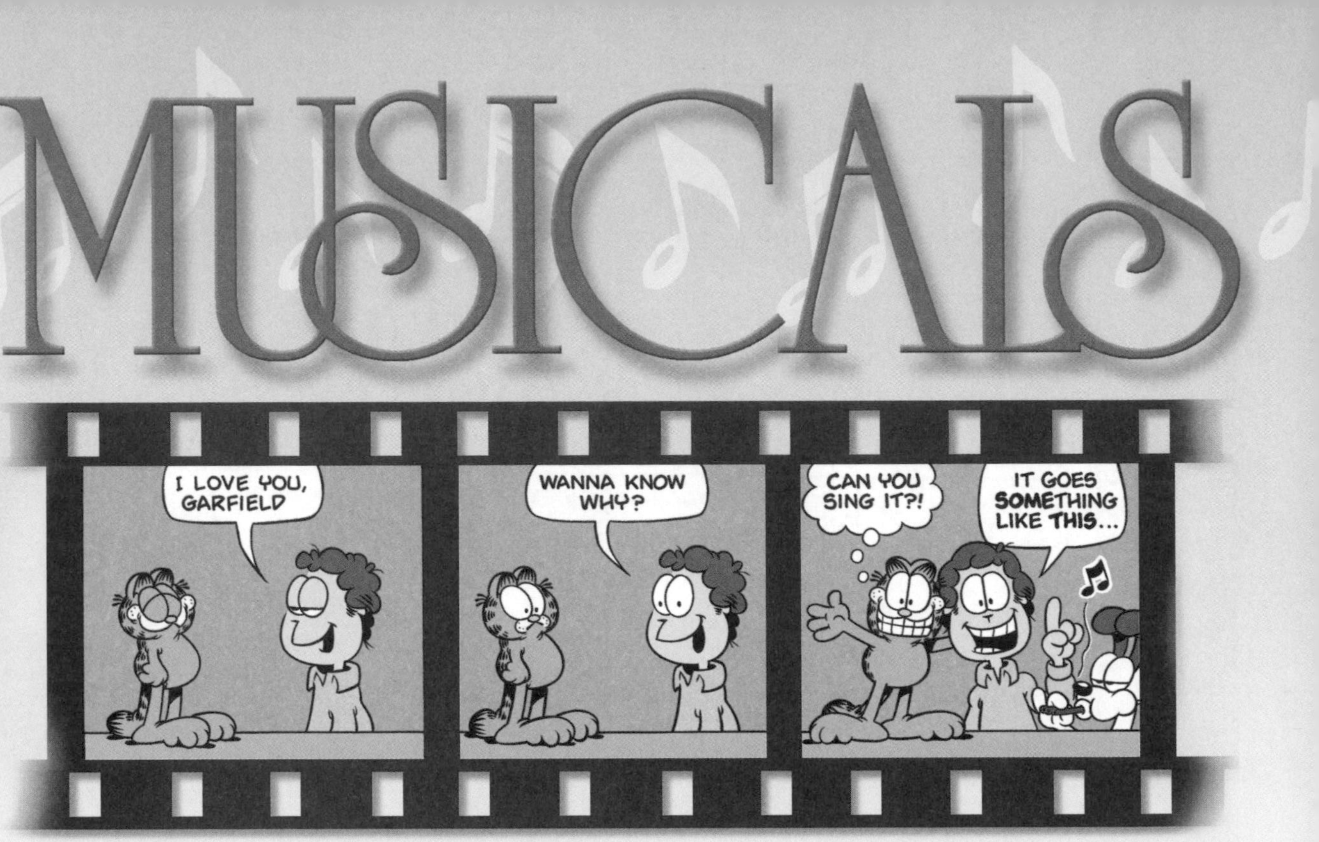
I LOVE YOU, GARFIELD
WANNA KNOW WHY?
CAN YOU SING IT?!
IT GOES SOMETHING LIKE THIS...

Truth be told, I like music better than musicals. I mean, I'm a natural-born entertainer who can croon and cavort with the best of 'em. But all that dancing, prancing, and, particularly, bursting into song in the middle of a scene can be a bit distracting. I feel like I'm sitting on a volcano that can erupt at any minute, spewing rhythmical and lyrical lava across the screen!

However, I still prefer movie musicals to the live stage. If I have to take a bathroom break during *The Wiz*, I just get up and go. And I can chomp chips and burp without the actors actually hearing me.

But don't get me wrong: I really do like some musicals. What kittenhood would be complete without the "supercalifragilisticexpialidocious" *Mary Poppins*? And the star-crossed teens lovin' it up in *West Side Story*—that's gangs of fun.

Bottom line is musicals are like vegetables: There's a cornucopia of shapes and sizes, and some are more palatable than others. Me, I don't do kale or broccoli like *Glitter*; yet, I will occasionally take in an Indian musical (with some curried potatoes and peas). Hooray for Bollywood! That's no song and dance—that's just the musically adventurous kind of cat I am.

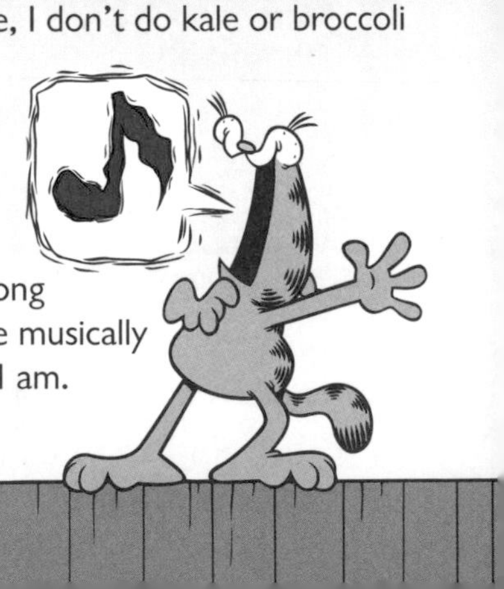

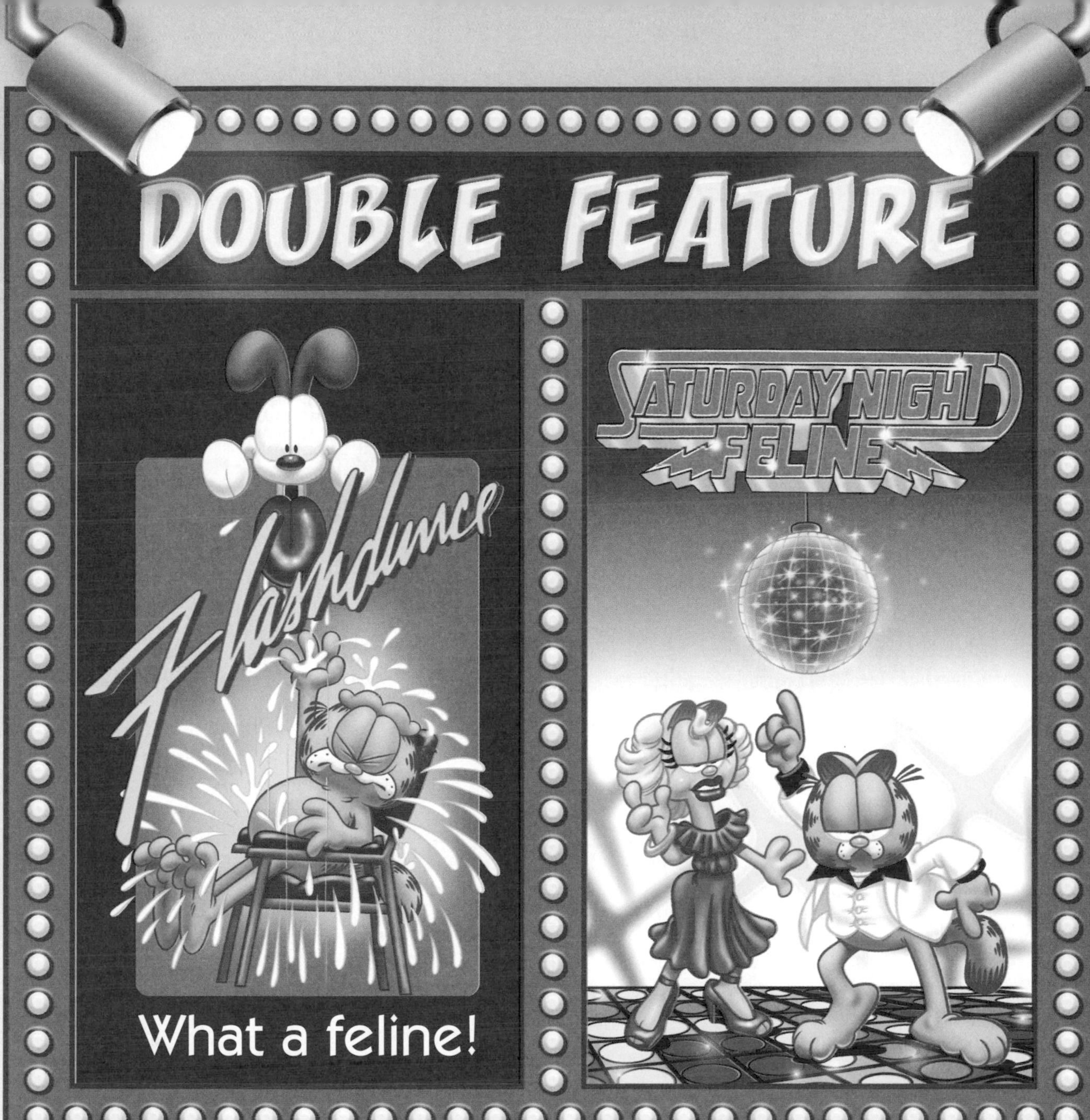
DOUBLE FEATURE
Flashdance
What a feline!
SATURDAY NIGHT FELINE

Romance

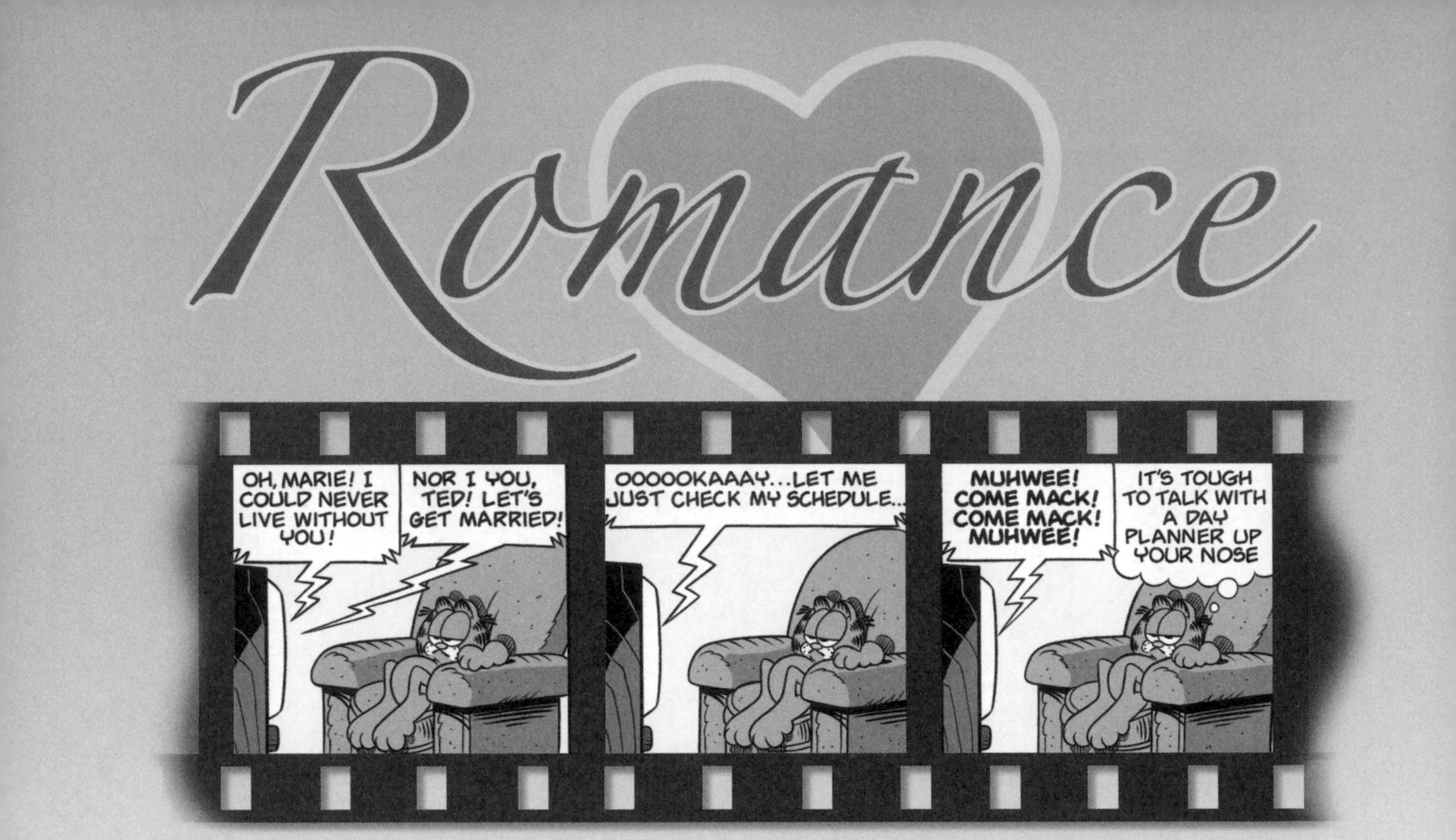

OH, MARIE! I COULD NEVER LIVE WITHOUT YOU!
NOR I YOU, TED! LET'S GET MARRIED!
OOOOOKAAAAY...LET ME JUST CHECK MY SCHEDULE...
MUHWEE! COME MACK! COME MACK! MUHWEE!
IT'S TOUGH TO TALK WITH A DAY PLANNER UP YOUR NOSE

Some call them "chick flicks." I call them "boring!" Maybe I'm just an unsentimental slob, but films about the guy getting the girl just never did anything for me. Now the guy getting the lasagna—and maybe some garlic bread on the side—*that's* my kind of love story.

Romantic movies seem to fall into two categories: The first is when two people find each other, fall in love, lose each other, find each other again, and live happily ever after (think *Jerry Maguire*). The second is when two people find each other, fall in love, and then one of them dies (think *Love Story*).

Both types of films elicit the same audience response: crying. People cry when the movie is happy. They cry when the movie is sad. I don't get it. The only time I cry in the theater is when Jon refuses to get me a refill on my tub of popcorn (and when he eats the last Milk Dud).

They say "Love means never having to say you're sorry." Forget that. I say, "Love means never having to say you're hungry."

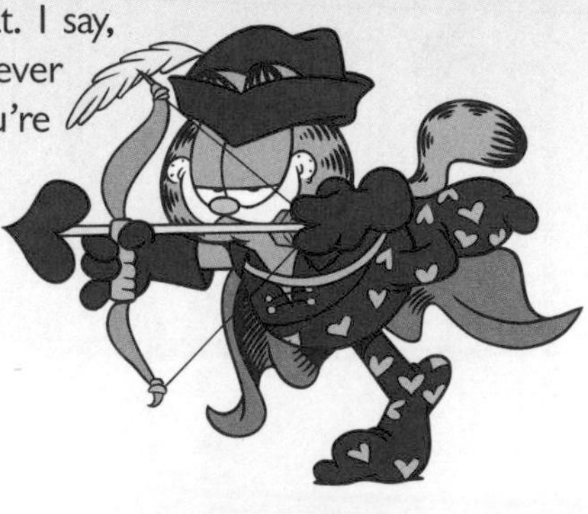

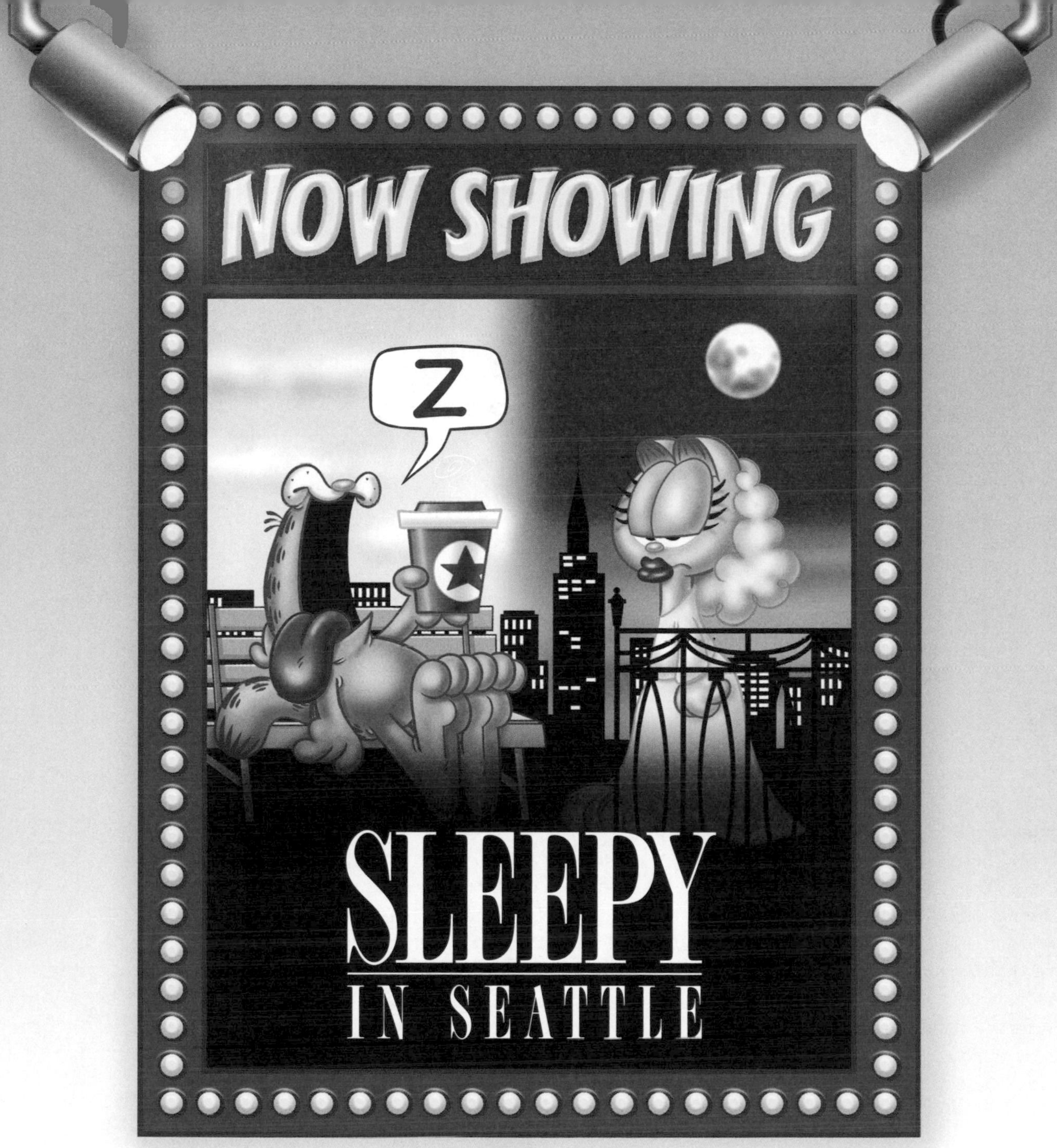
NOW SHOWING
Z
SLEEPY
IN SEATTLE

Science✷Fiction

AND NOW, THE STORY OF A WARM AND LOVING CAT

...ON "SCIENCE FICTION THEATER!"

WEIRD

CLICK

Back in the old days (read the 1950s and '60s), sci-fi films were low-budget B-movies with bad stories and worse special effects. But they did have great titles. Check out these gems of the genre: *Attack of the Crab Monsters; Cat Women of the Moon; The Brain That Wouldn't Die; Zombies of the Stratosphere; The Leech Woman; Attack of the Puppet People; The Killer Shrews; Santa Claus Conquers the Martians; Mars Needs Women; Zontar, the Thing from Venus;* and the best worst movie ever made—Ed Wood's *Plan 9 from Outer Space*.

Sure, the "science" in these movies was pretty shaky, but who could resist bug-eyed aliens, flying saucers, and giant radioactive insects? Speaking of big bugs, the 1955 flick

Tarantula, about an oversized spider, always gave me the creeps. My answer to that movie would be *Attack of the 50-Foot Newspaper*. But I digress . . .

When *Star Wars* blasted into theaters in 1977, it made money at warp speed, and Hollywood has been in love with science fiction ever since. Along with the multiple sequels and prequels to Lucas's space saga, we have the *Terminator* films, the *Alien* films, the *Predator* films—even *Alien Versus Predator*. What's next? How about *Alien and Predator Versus Terminator and Darth Vader on the Planet of the Apes*. I'd buy a ticket to *that*!

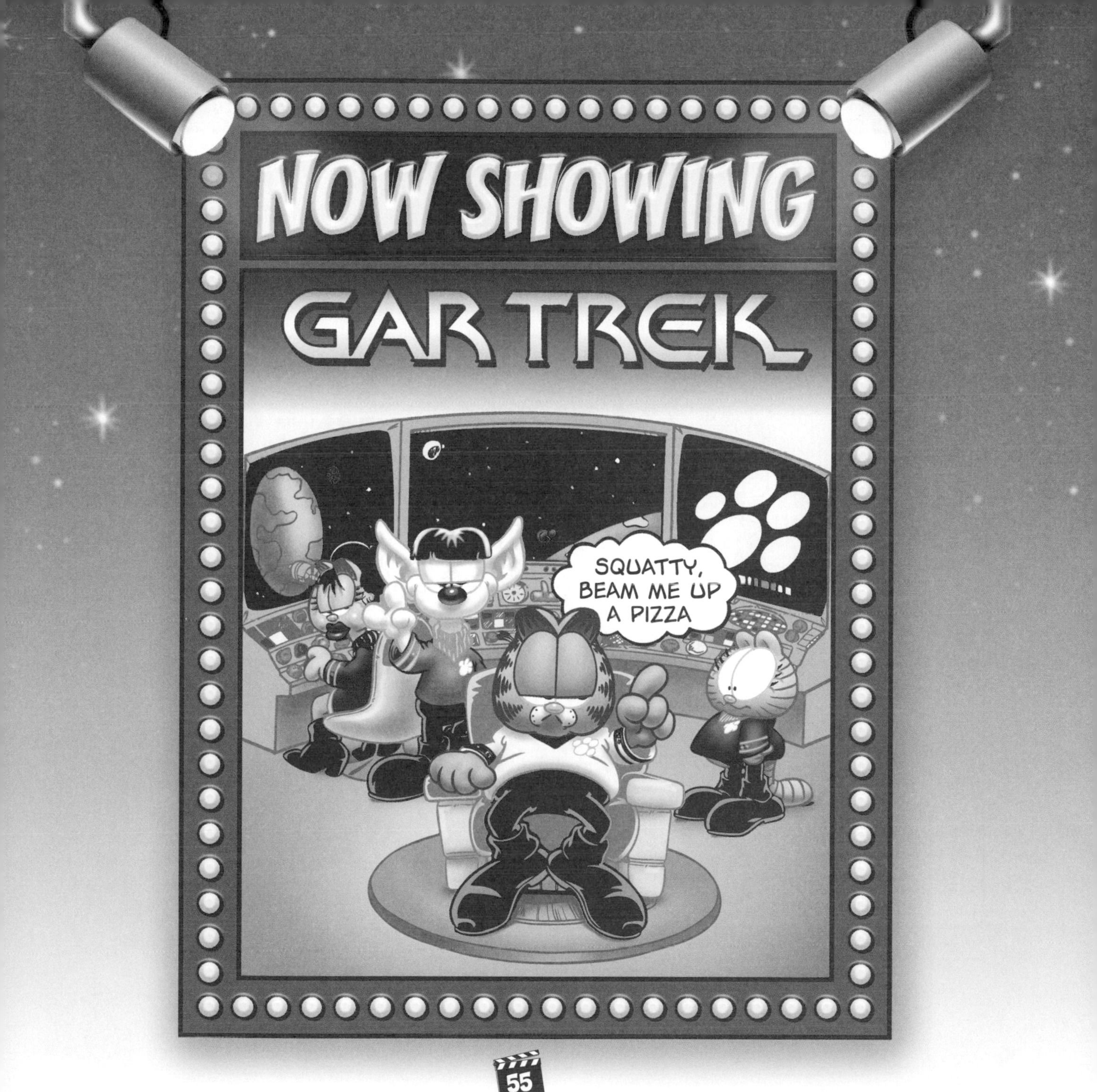
NOW SHOWING
GAR TREK
SQUATTY, BEAM ME UP A PIZZA

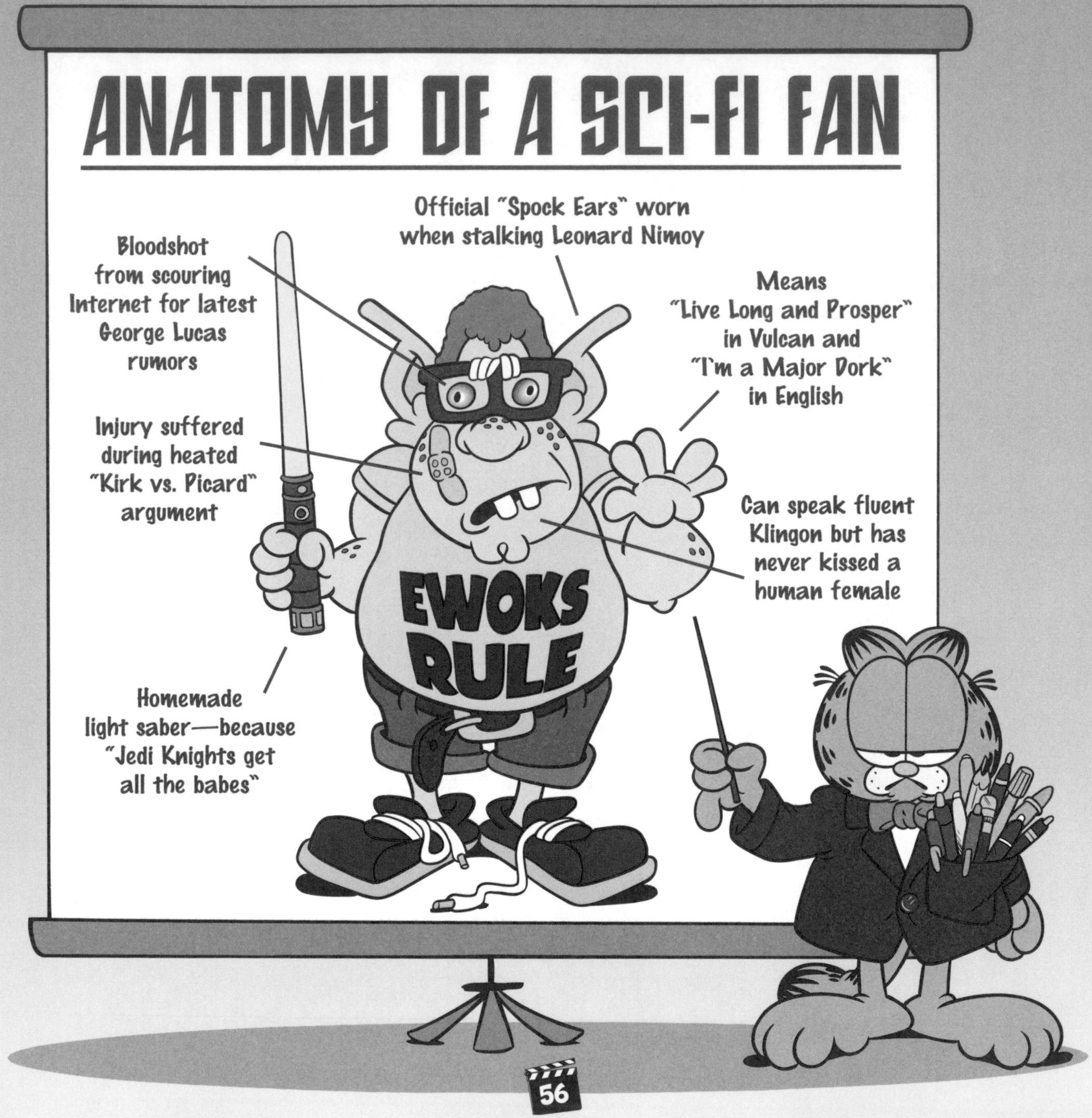
ANATOMY OF A SCI-FI FAN
Official "Spock Ears" worn when stalking Leonard Nimoy
Bloodshot from scouring Internet for latest George Lucas rumors
Means "Live Long and Prosper" in Vulcan and "I'm a Major Dork" in English
Injury suffered during heated "Kirk vs. Picard" argument
Can speak fluent Klingon but has never kissed a human female
EWOKS RULE
Homemade light saber—because "Jedi Knights get all the babes"

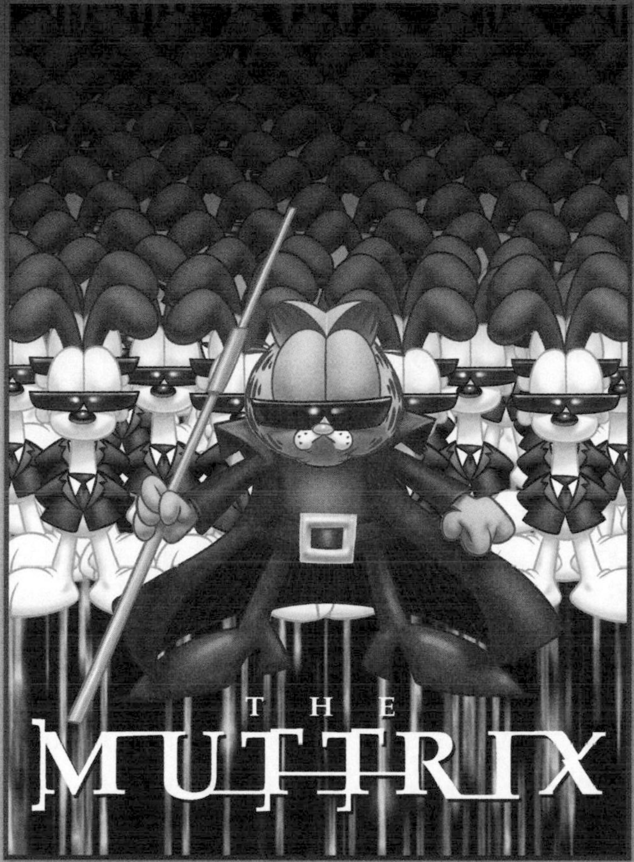
THE
MUTTRIX

🐾🐾🐾🐾🐾 A visual slice of heaven 🐾🐾🐾🐾 A "reel" treat
🐾🐾🐾 Worth a taste 🐾🐾 Barely palatable 🐾 Gagger

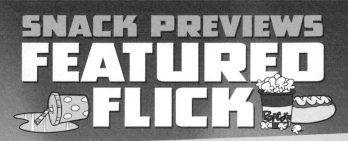

SNACK PREVIEWS FEATURED FLICK

THE GOOD:
Two words—"Bullet Time!"

THE BAD:
Convoluted plot made me sprain my brain. ("There is no spoon." Huh?)

THE SCORE:
🐾 🐾 🐾

"What is the Muttrix? Who the heck knows—but the action is awesome!"

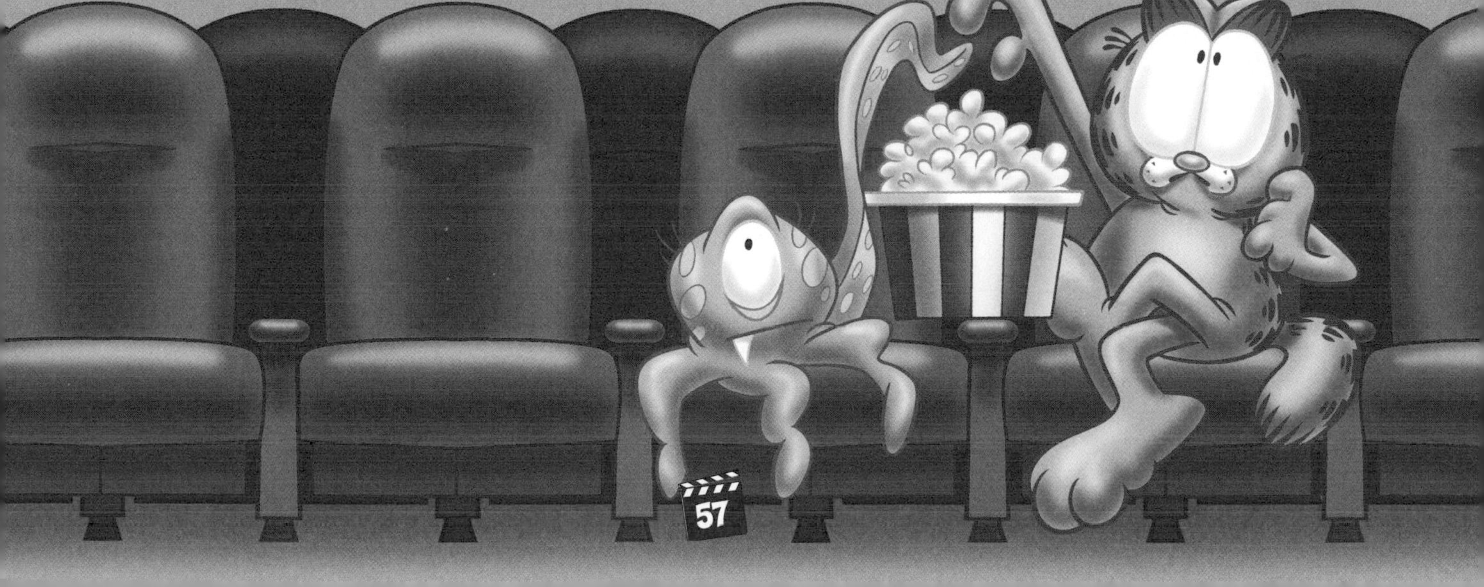

SILENT

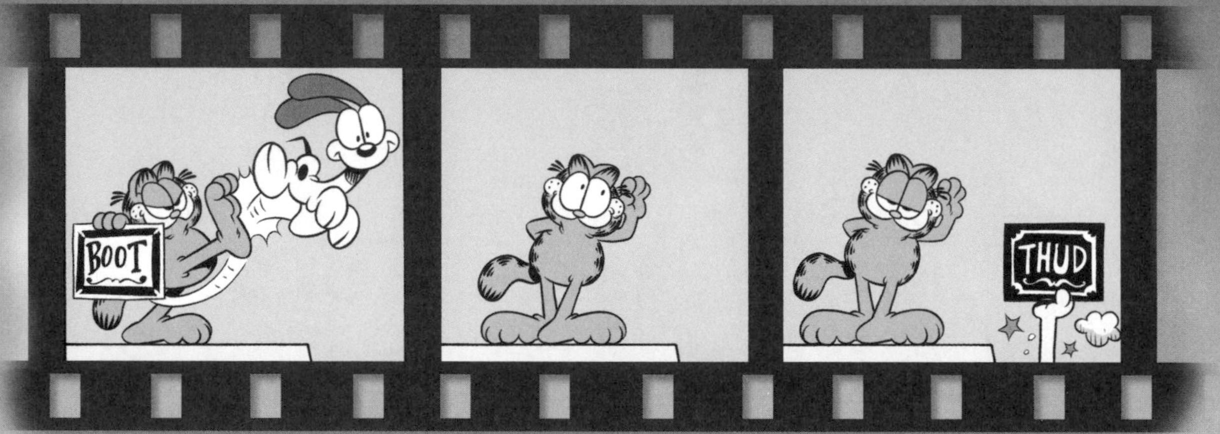
BOOT
THUD

"We didn't need dialogue. We had faces!" Gloria Swanson (as Norma Desmond) said that in *Sunset Boulevard*, Billy Wilder's spellbinding drama about a faded silent-era movie star.

I'm not sure I totally agree. After all, I'm known for my snappy dialogue—as well as my impressive physique (hey, don't laugh!). But the films made before the late 1920s when sound revolutionized motion pictures are pretty darn impressive. Clara Bow (the "It" girl), Mary Pickford, Gloria Swanson, Douglas Fairbanks, Rudolph Valentino, and a personal fave, Lon Chaney, the man of a thousand faces, lit up those early movie screens in a way not seen since. Millions of fans flocked to theaters each week to see their favorite stars in larger-than-life epics.

The silent era was also the golden age of movie comedy. Charlie Chaplin, Buster Keaton, Harold Lloyd—these comic giants were masters of slapstick and inspired generations of funnymen (and -women). I do my small part to keep the spirit of slapstick alive . . . every time I boot Odie off the table.

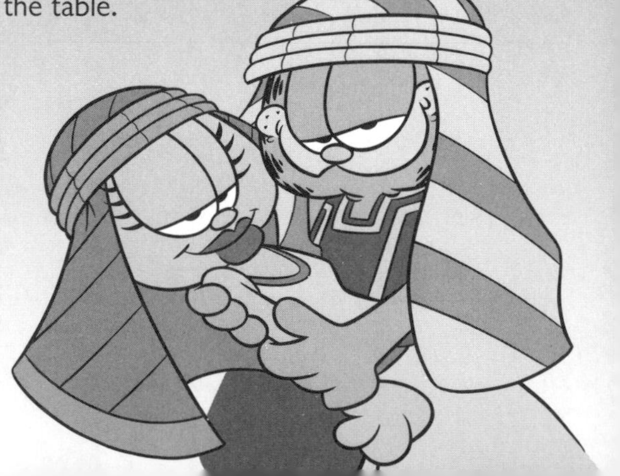

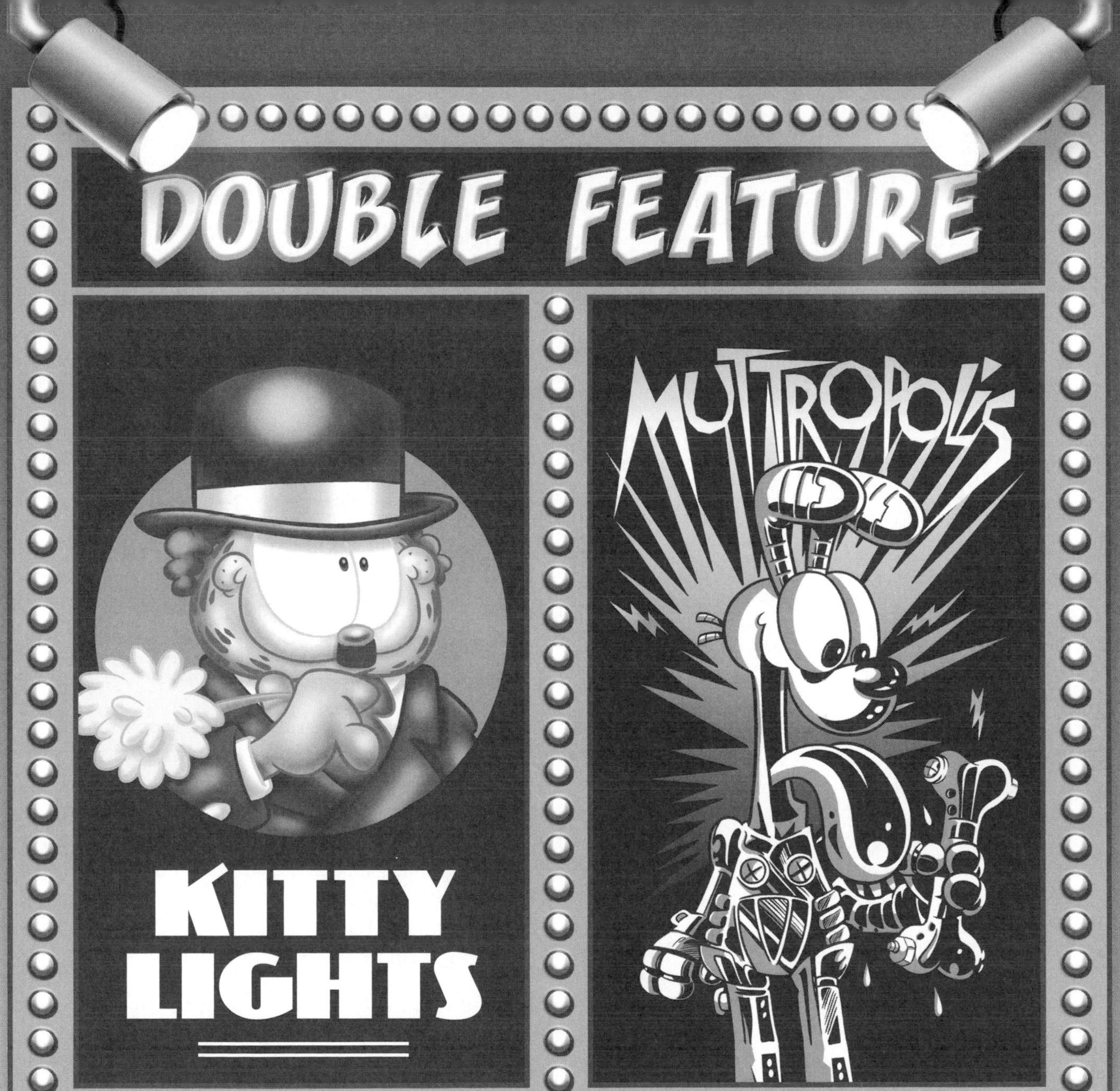
DOUBLE FEATURE
KITTY LIGHTS
MUTTROPOLIS

SPORTS

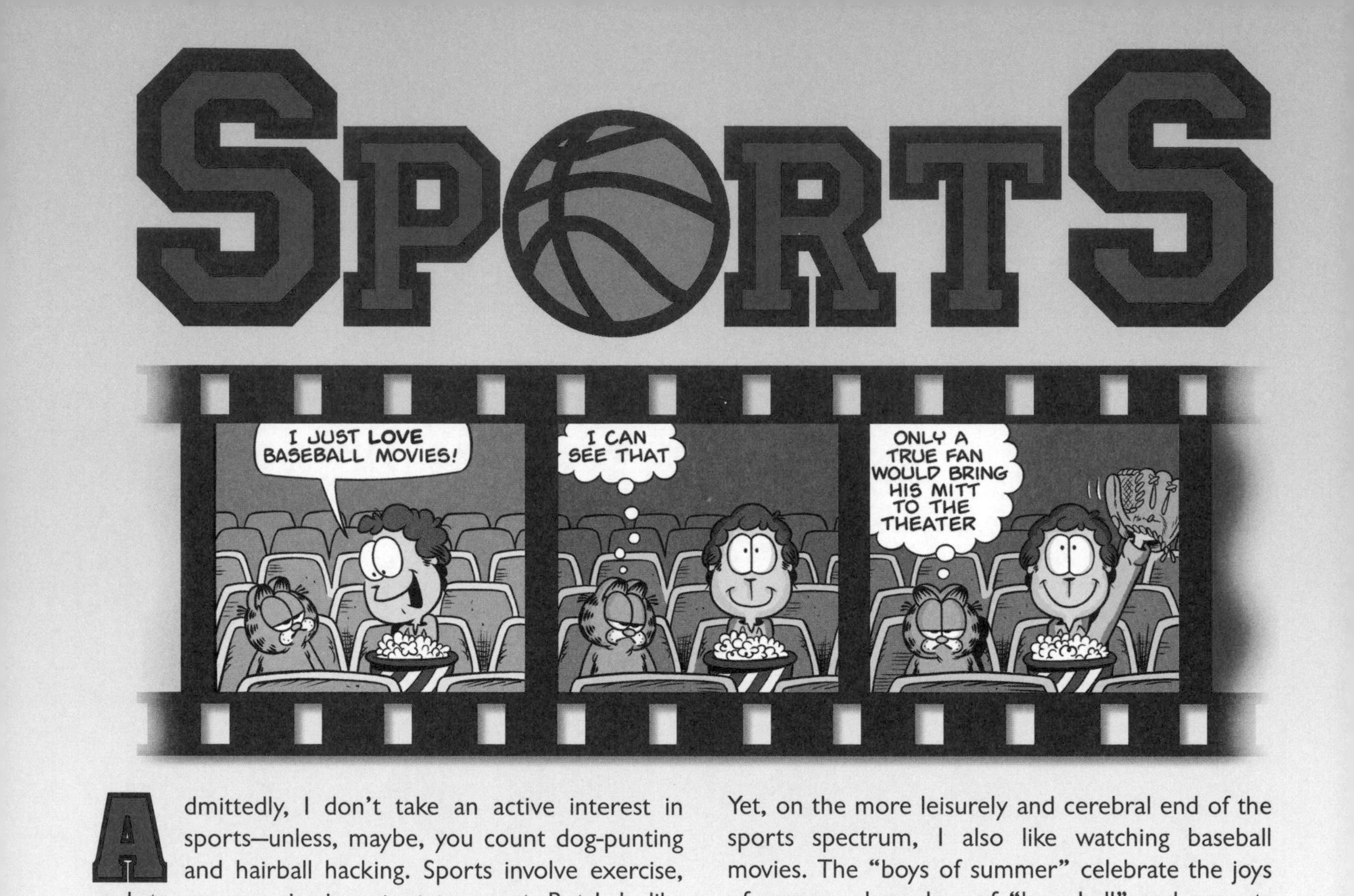
I JUST LOVE BASEBALL MOVIES!
I CAN SEE THAT
ONLY A TRUE FAN WOULD BRING HIS MITT TO THE THEATER

Admittedly, I don't take an active interest in sports—unless, maybe, you count dog-punting and hairball hacking. Sports involve exercise, and, to me, exercise is a *spectator* sport. But I do like to channel surf and catch a sports flick on the tube now and then. And I mean real sports films, not ones about figure skating, rowing, or chess. Puh-leeze.

I prefer the head-pounding pleasures of boxing movies such as *Raging Bull* or *Rocky*. I get so caught up in the action that I use Odie as a punching bag and believe I could become heavyweight champ of the world. Of course, then I remember I have a "glass jowl" and hate shedding blood—especially my own.

Yet, on the more leisurely and cerebral end of the sports spectrum, I also like watching baseball movies. The "boys of summer" celebrate the joys of summer—lazy days of "long ball" and peanuts and Cracker Jacks. (I especially enjoy the seventh-inning snack followed by the eighth-inning nap.) I like both comedies (*Bull Durham*) and dramas (*The Natural*). But I don't like when the Bad News Bears go to Japan or Kazakhstan or wherever.

And what, pray tell, is my least favorite sports film of all time? It's gotta be that sappy pooch-hoopin' *Air Bud*. That movie was a dog!

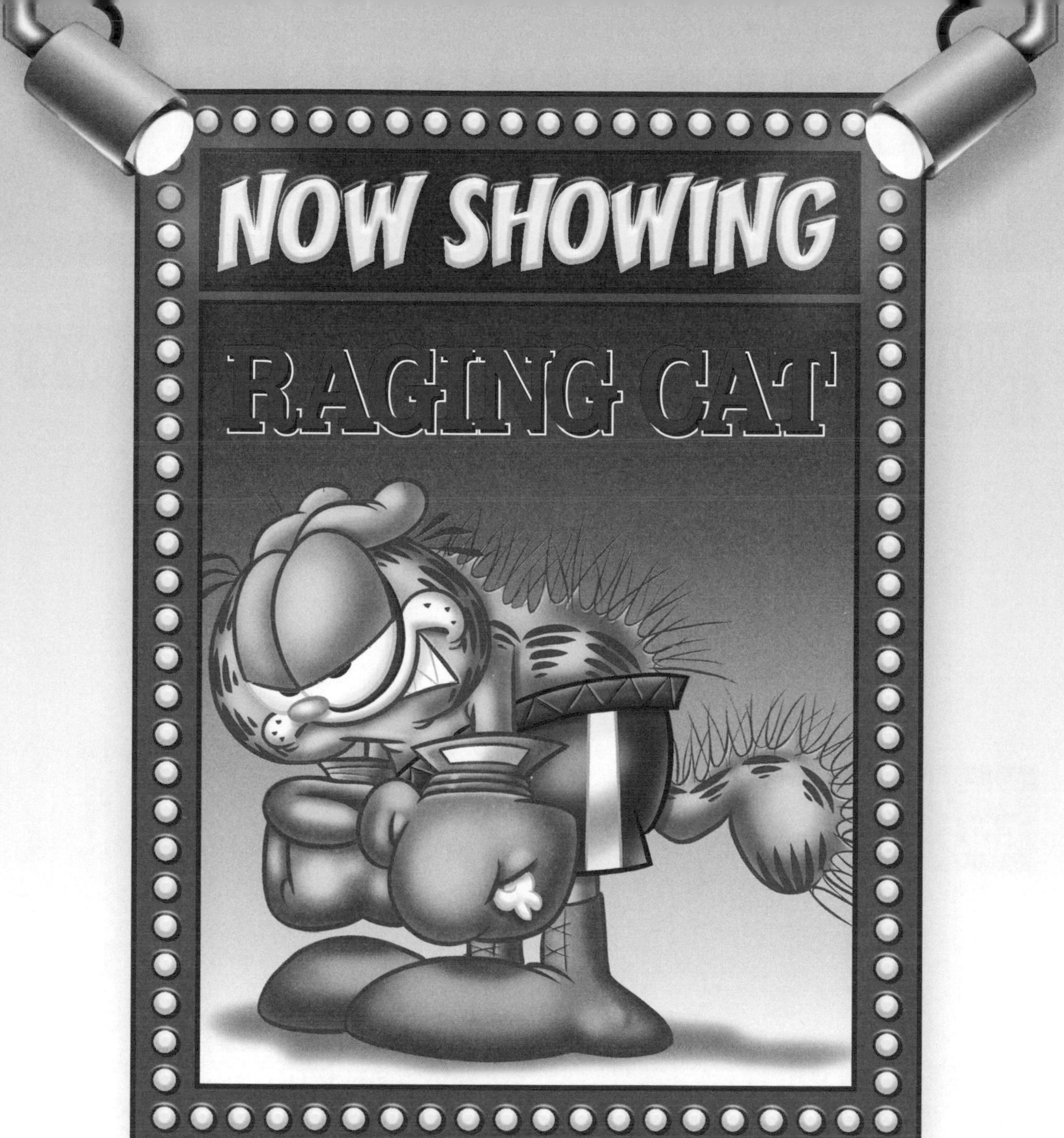
NOW SHOWING
RAGING CAT

SPORTS MOVIES THAT DIDN'T SCORE WELL

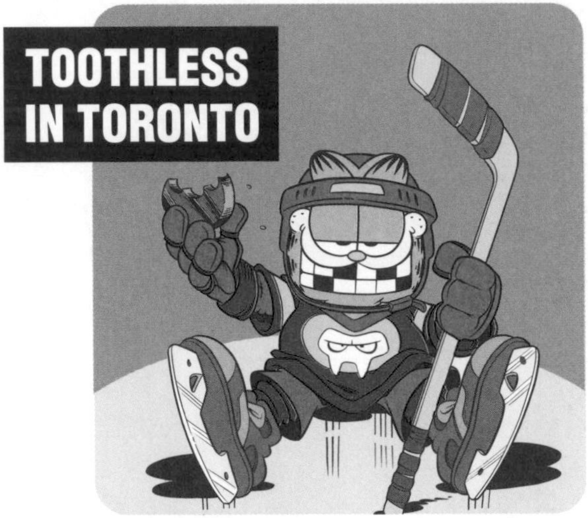
TOOTHLESS IN TORONTO

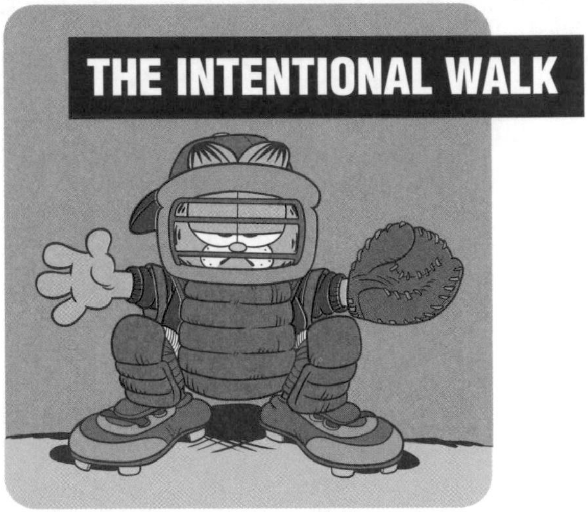
THE INTENTIONAL WALK

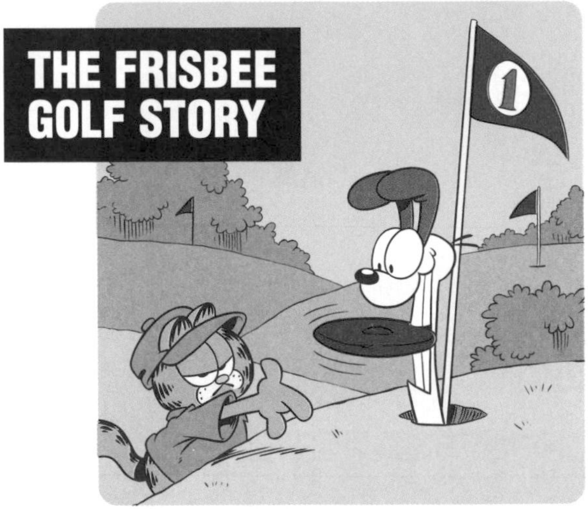
THE FRISBEE GOLF STORY
1

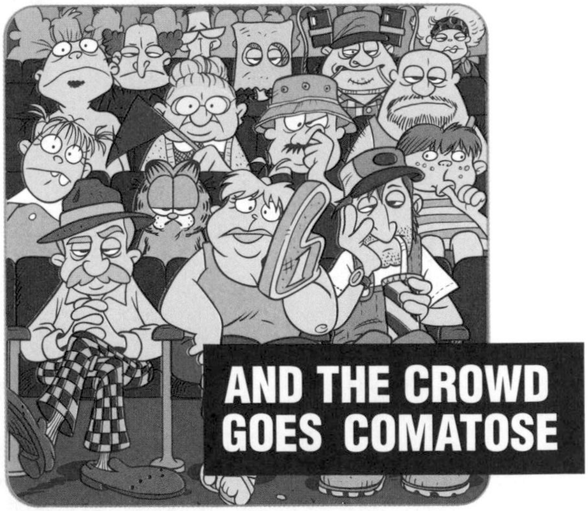
AND THE CROWD GOES COMATOSE

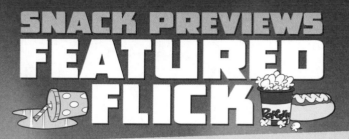

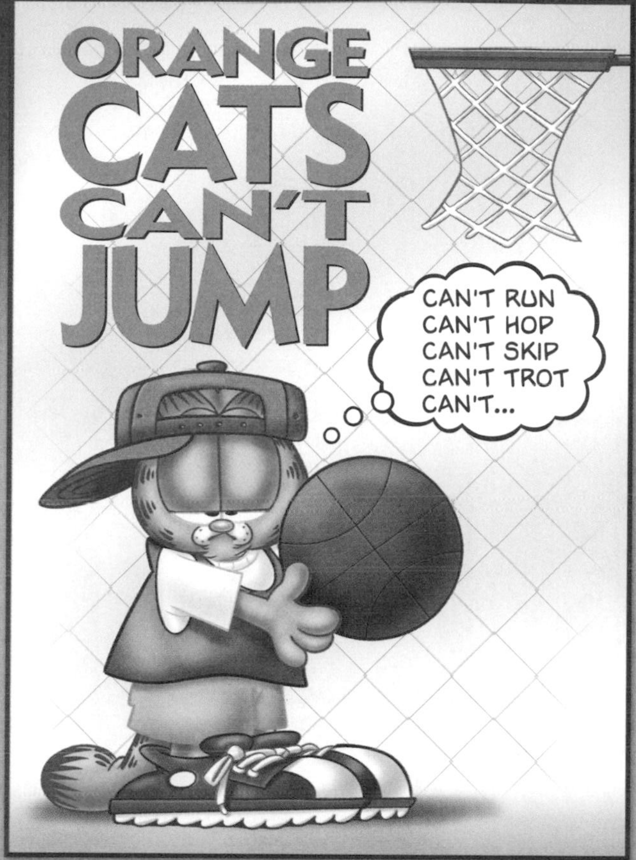
ORANGE CATS CAN'T JUMP
CAN'T RUN
CAN'T HOP
CAN'T SKIP
CAN'T TROT
CAN'T...

A visual slice of heaven A "reel" treat
Worth a taste Barely palatable Gagger

SNACK PREVIEWS FEATURED FLICK

THE GOOD:
Too much "trash talk" is never enough.

THE BAD:
Contrived ending in jeopardy of being unbelievable.

THE SCORE:

"Hairball comedy hoops it up!"

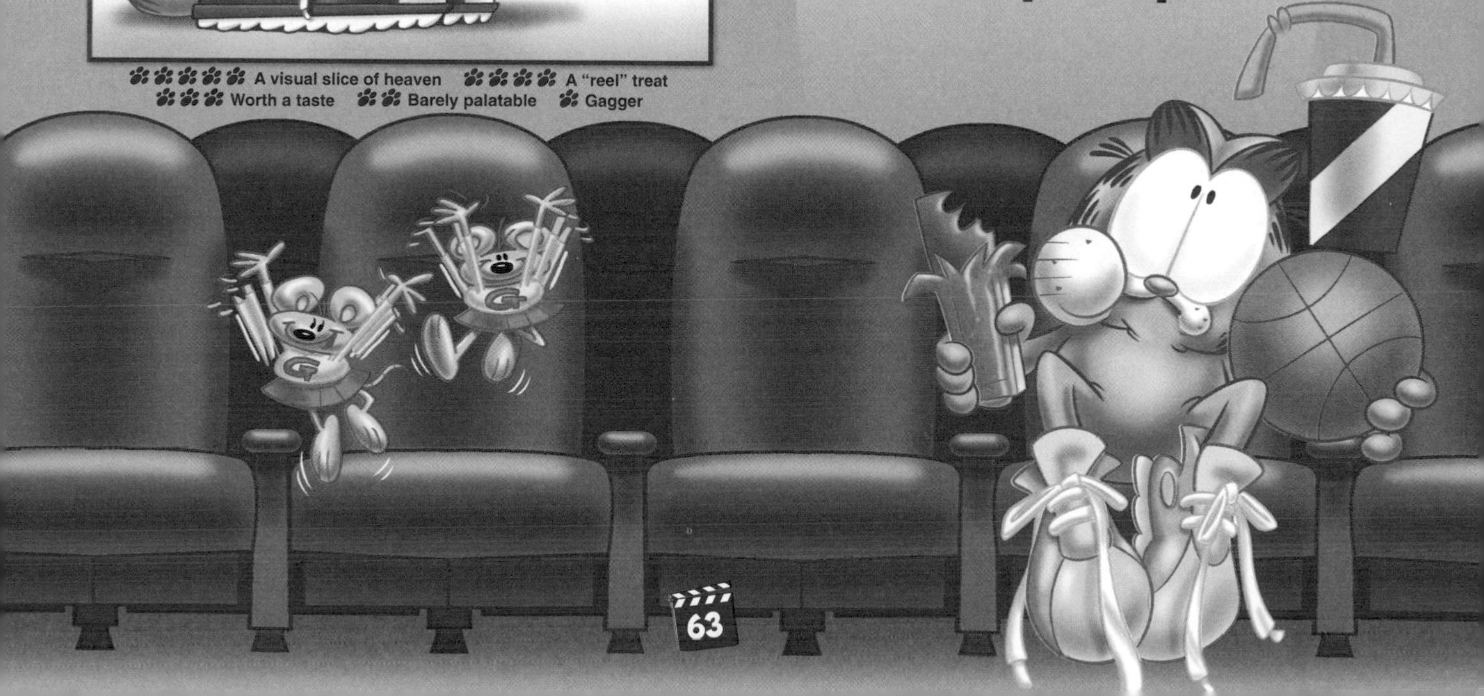

SUPERHERO

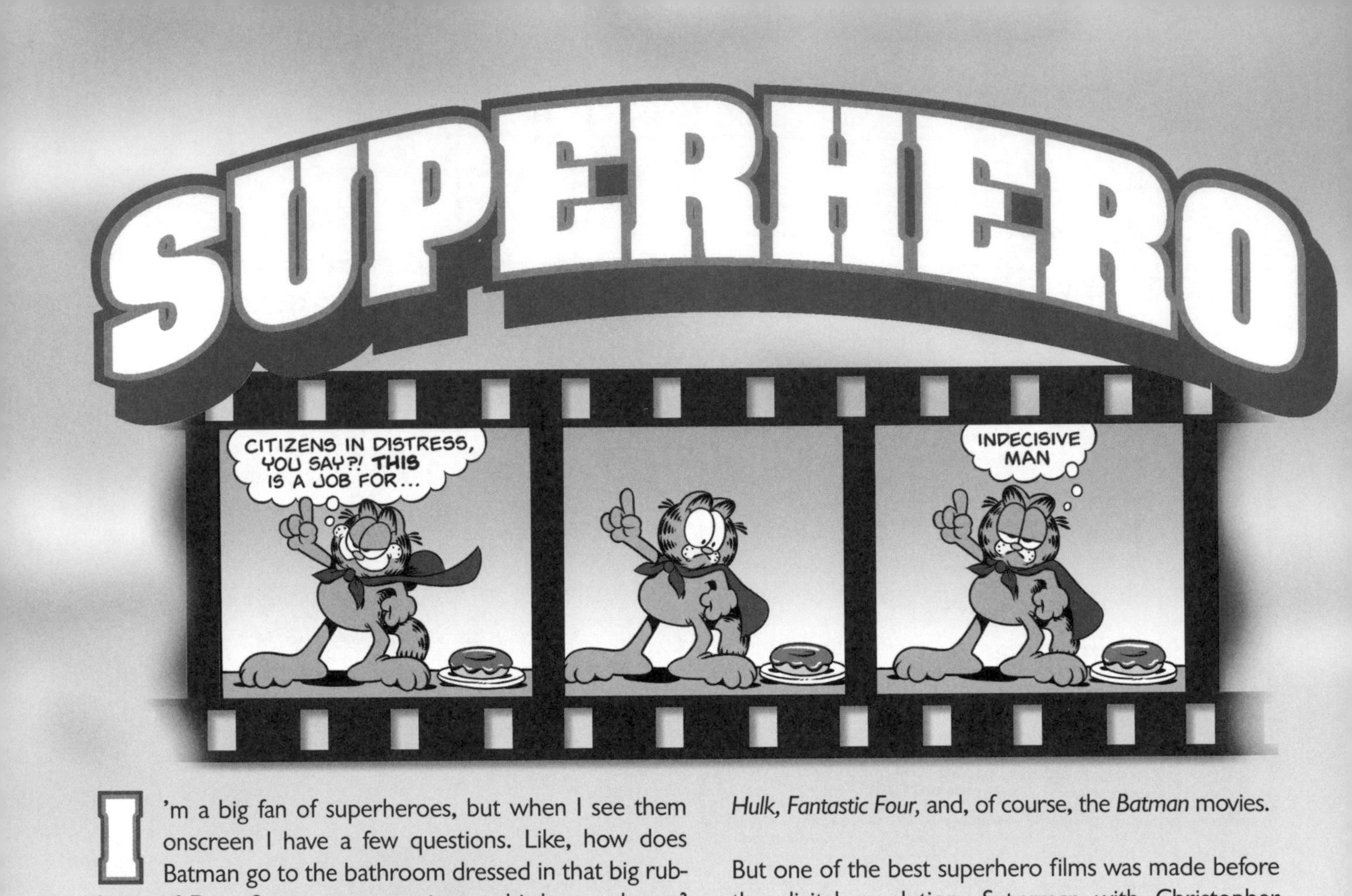
CITIZENS IN DISTRESS, YOU SAY?! THIS IS A JOB FOR...
INDECISIVE MAN

I'm a big fan of superheroes, but when I see them onscreen I have a few questions. Like, how does Batman go to the bathroom dressed in that big rubber suit? Does Superman ever trip over his long red cape? And what's up with the Hulk's pants? A scrawny guy changes into a 15-foot Goliath and shreds every stitch of clothing except his trousers? What are they made of, and can I get some of that material for a scratching post?

Superhero films are currently enjoying something of a renaissance—thanks in large part to the magic of CGI. Computer effects have helped the heroes become truly super in such fun flicks as *X-Men, Spider-Man, Daredevil, The Hulk, Fantastic Four,* and, of course, the *Batman* movies.

But one of the best superhero films was made before the digital revolution. *Superman* with Christopher Reeve hit theaters in 1978. The ads promised "you will believe a man can fly." And we did. What we couldn't believe was that Marlon Brando got paid three million bucks to read a handful of lines off a cue card.

Superman treated the superhero with respect and dignity. Well, as much dignity as you can have when you're flying around in a red-and-blue leotard. Which makes me wonder: Did he ever get a wedgie in midflight?

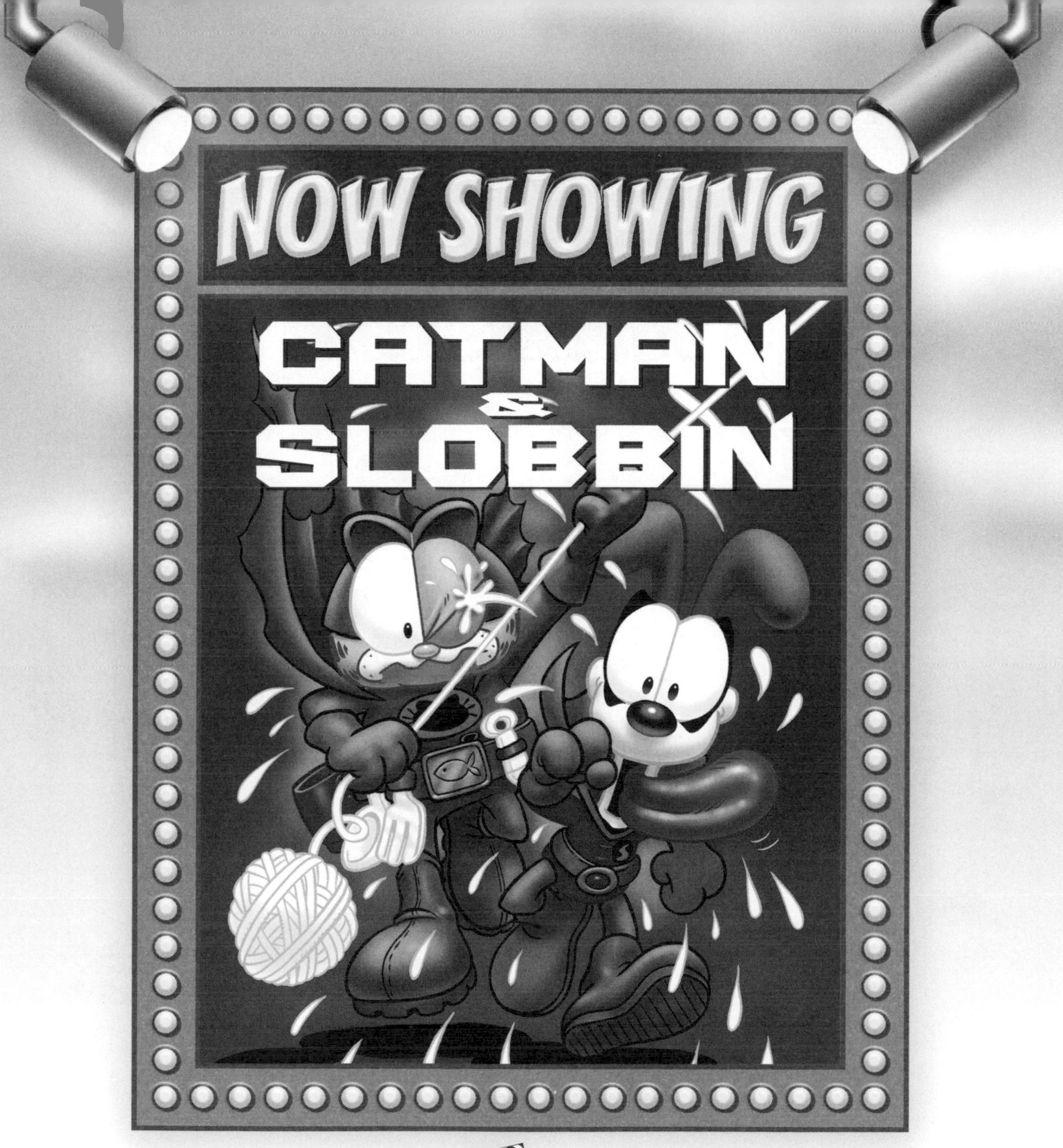
NOW SHOWING
CATMAN
&
SLOBBIN

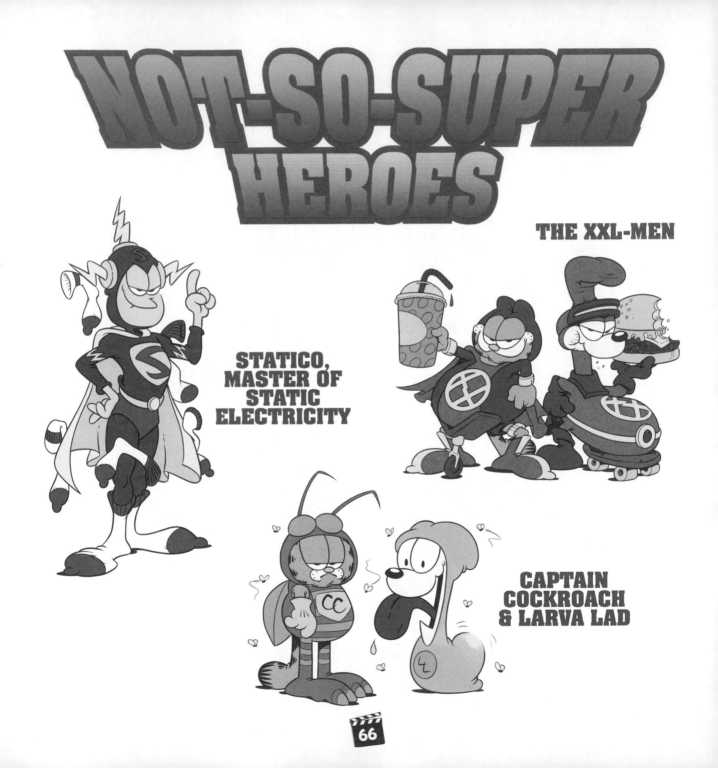

NOT-SO-SUPER HEROES

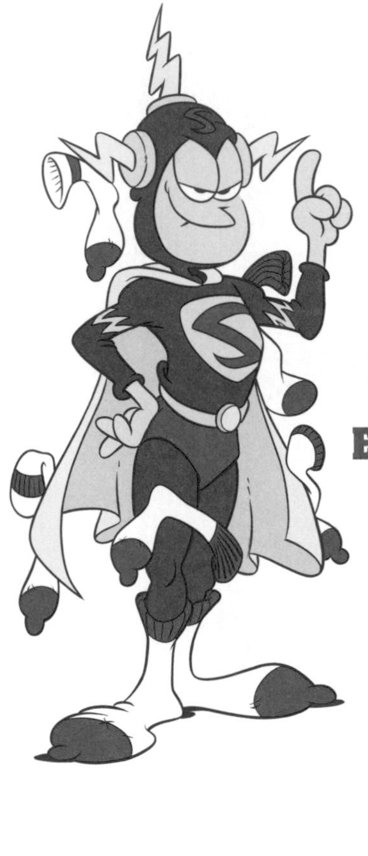

STATICO, MASTER OF STATIC ELECTRICITY

THE XXL-MEN

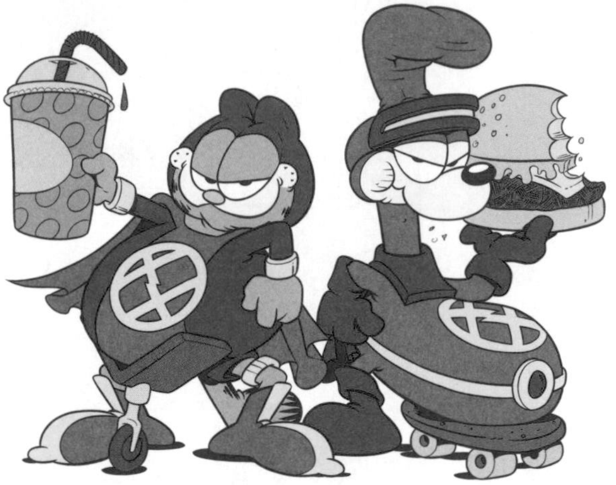

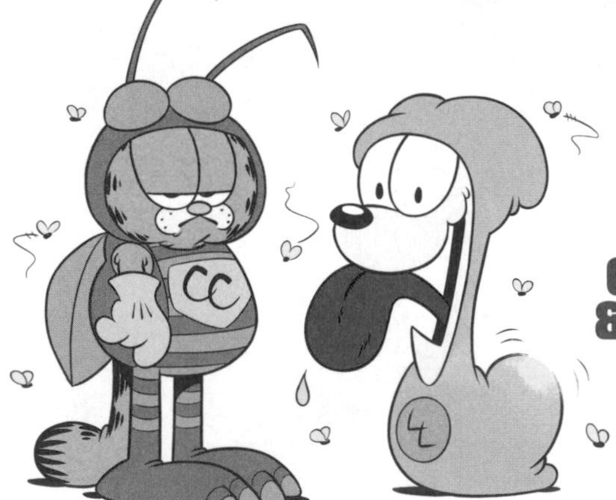

CAPTAIN COCKROACH & LARVA LAD

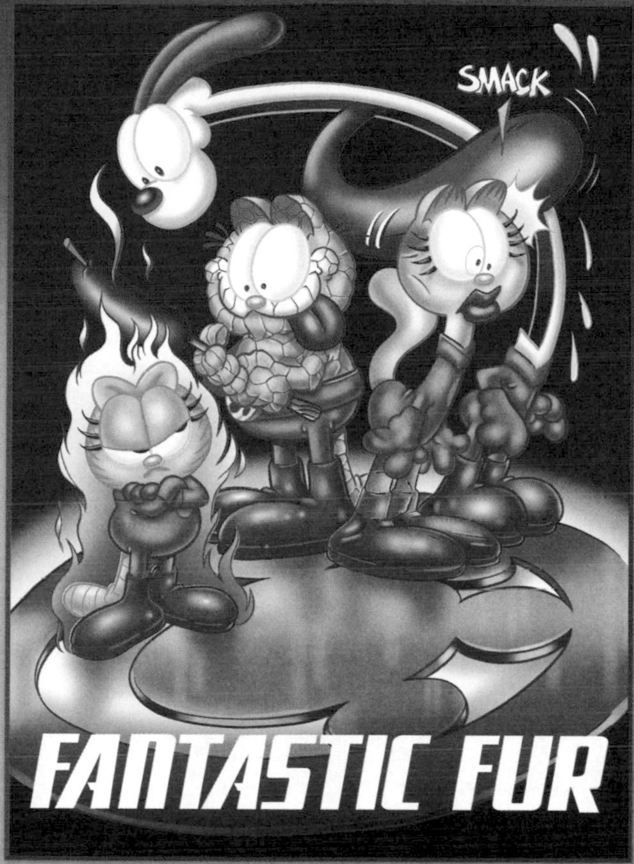
SMACK
FANTASTIC FUR

5 paws: A visual slice of heaven · 4 paws: A "reel" treat · 3 paws: Worth a taste · 2 paws: Barely palatable · 1 paw: Gagger

SNACK PREVIEWS FEATURED FLICK

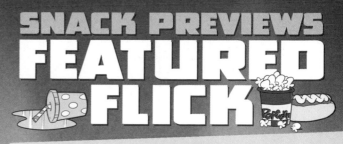

THE GOOD:
It's clobberin' time! The big orange guy and his hotheaded teammate save the day (and the film!).

THE BAD:
Leader of team (and the arch-villain) not so fantastic.

THE SCORE:
(3 paws)

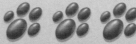

"They may not be incredible—but this foursome lives up to its name."

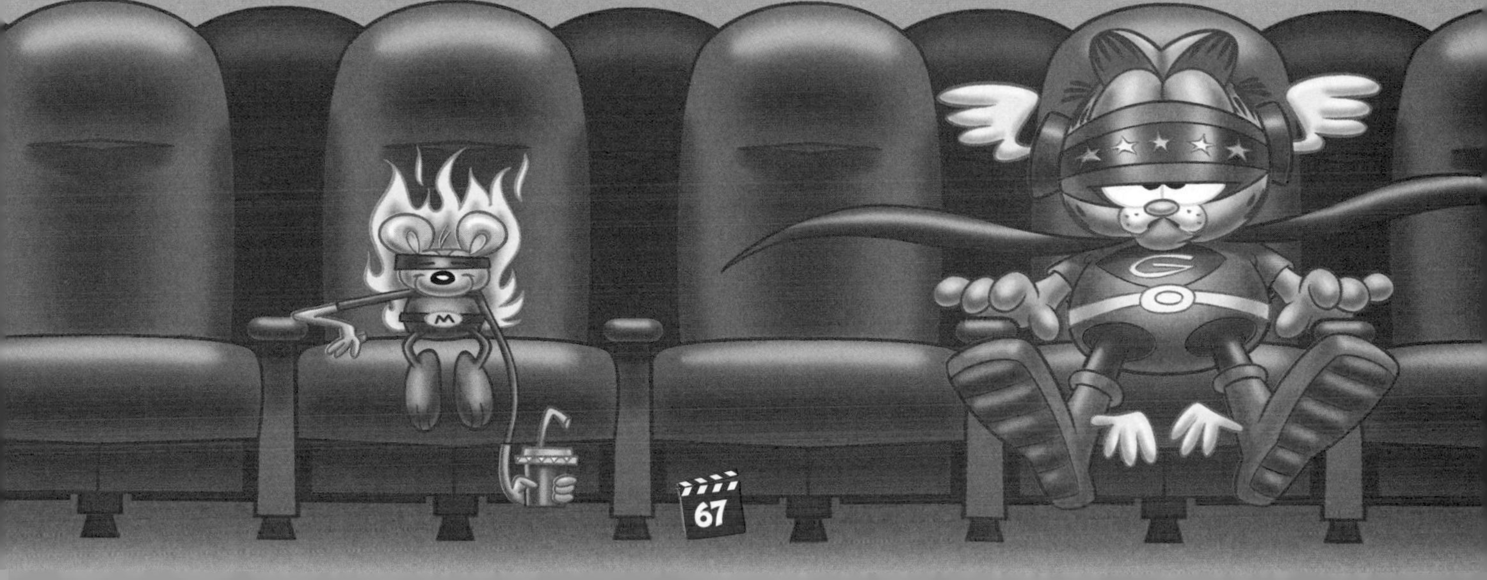

Teen

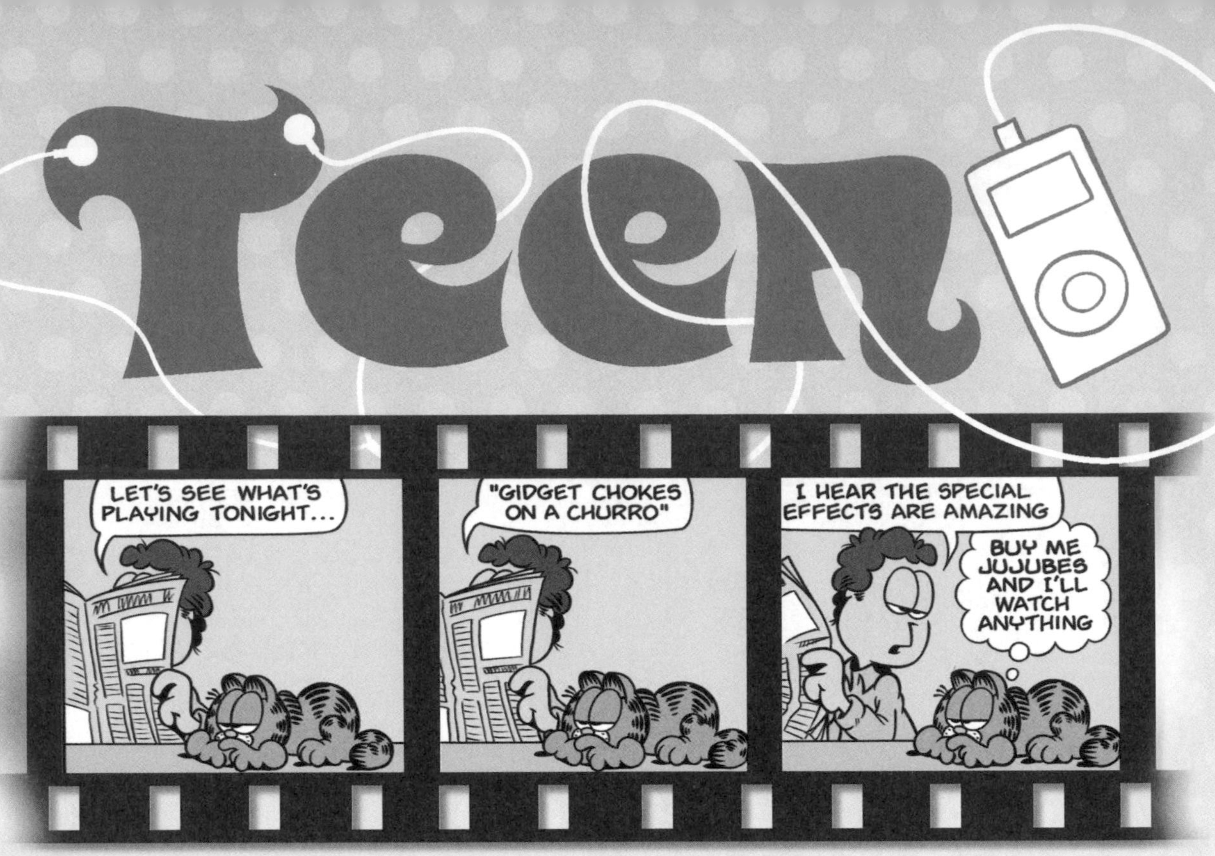
LET'S SEE WHAT'S PLAYING TONIGHT...
"GIDGET CHOKES ON A CHURRO"
I HEAR THE SPECIAL EFFECTS ARE AMAZING
BUY ME JUJUBES AND I'LL WATCH ANYTHING

Ah, teen movies: the junk food of cinema. Sure they're chock-full of clichéd characters and predictable situations, but they can still be satisfying—kind of like the movie equivalent of McDonald's: familiar, prepackaged fare for the less adventurous palate. (Hey! I'm making myself hungry again!)

Just in case you've never seen one of these cinematic masterpieces, here's a sample plot: A popular jock bets his friend that he can turn the plain-looking girl with the glasses into a prom queen. The girl, of course, miraculously transforms into a hottie once she removes her glasses, lets her hair down, and slips into a slinky party dress. (Hey, who needs "Extreme Makeover"?)

Teen "McMovies" also offer valuable wisdom, such as cheerleaders are evil; attractive foreign-exchange students will date you because they don't speak English; sometimes nerds can be cool; and the most important lesson of all: Never throw a party when your parents leave town because they will invariably return a day early and show up at precisely the same time as the local law enforcement.

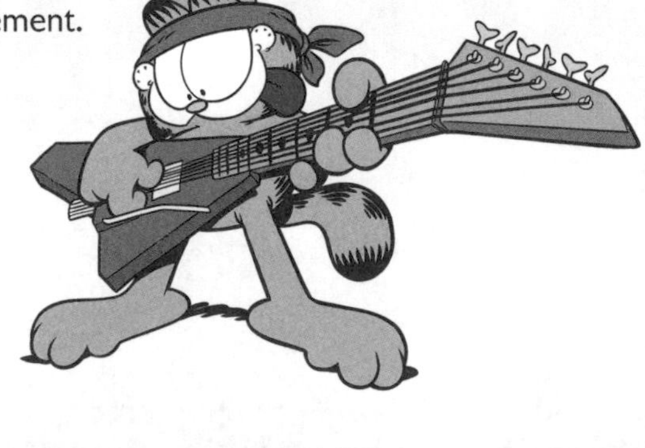

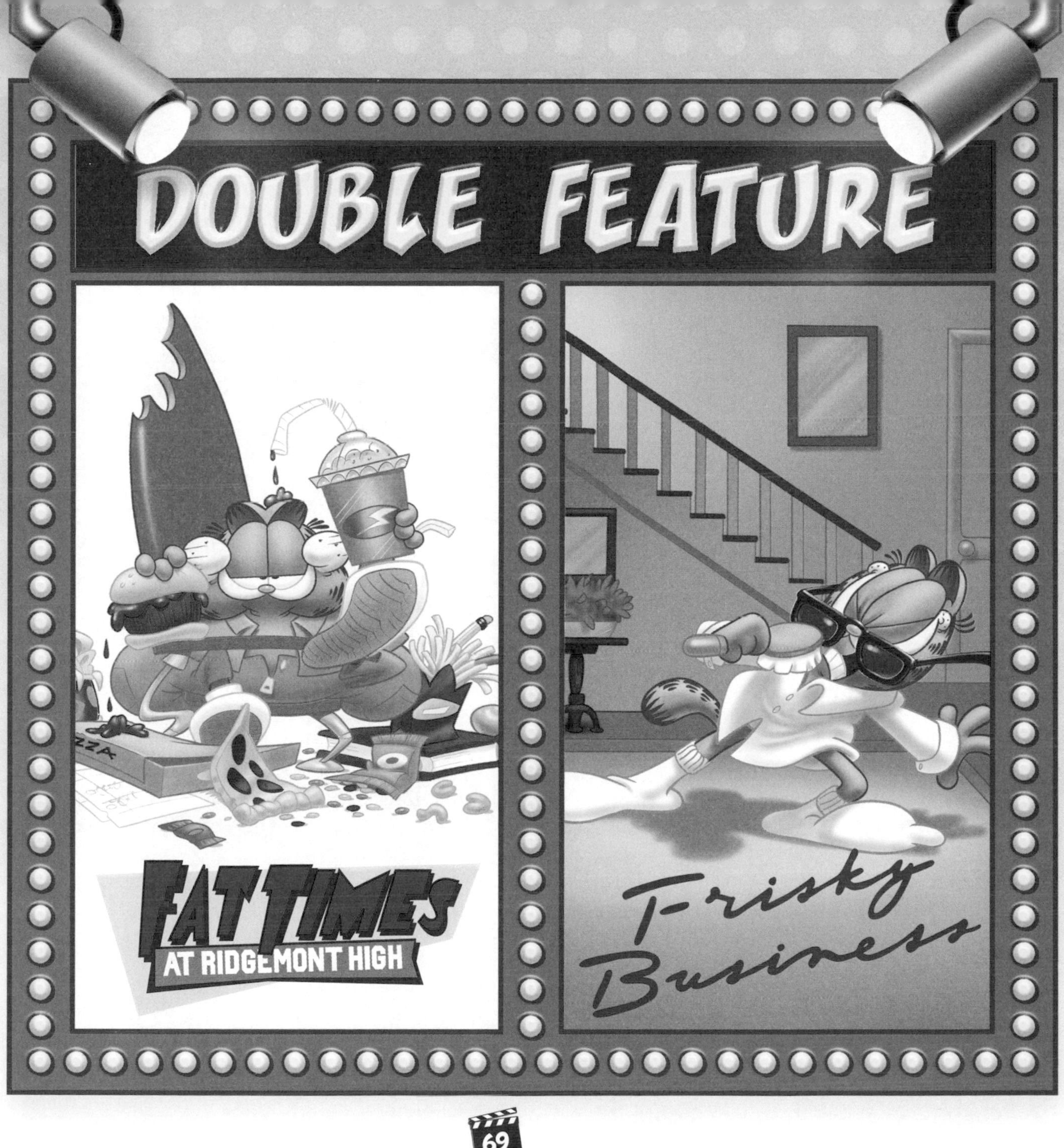
DOUBLE FEATURE
PIZZA
FAT TIMES
AT RIDGEMONT HIGH
Frisky
Business

WESTERNS

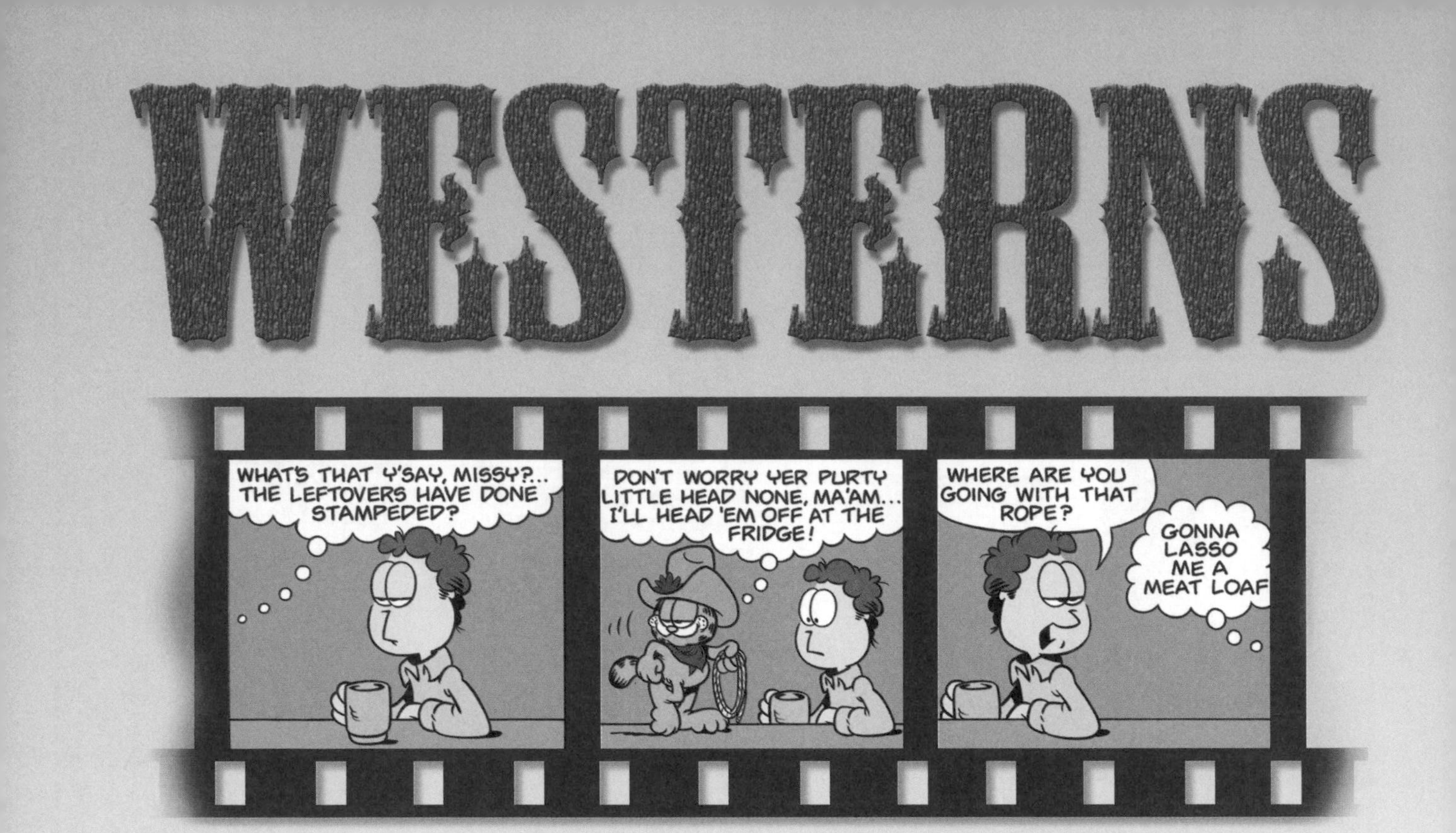
WHAT'S THAT Y'SAY, MISSY?... THE LEFTOVERS HAVE DONE STAMPEDED?
DON'T WORRY YER PURTY LITTLE HEAD NONE, MA'AM... I'LL HEAD 'EM OFF AT THE FRIDGE!
WHERE ARE YOU GOING WITH THAT ROPE?
GONNA LASSO ME A MEAT LOAF

I love a good rootin'-tootin', shoot-'em-up western! They're so colorful, even when they're in black and white. Gunslinging cowboys, marauding Indians, dance-hall girls, barroom brawls, galloping horses, stampeding cattle, train robberies, bank robberies . . . these westerns were the original action films. Yee-ha!

My favorite plot is one of the most basic: A stranger rides into town, kicks some black-hat, bad-guy butt, then rides off into the sunset, preferably *without* the girl. Let's face it: Our hero has enough problems trying to tame the wild frontier without some woman trying to tame *him*. I can relate: I'm too busy ridin' herd on the Arbuckle homestead and strappin' on the feedbag to let a lass lasso me.

My least faves are movies in which the Indians are treated like dogs (that's as low as it goes in my book). Historically, these *original* Americans have gotten savaged in what is the most American of all film genres. Cowboy hats off to *Dances with Wolves* for empathizing with the Indians in a new brand of western.

But, pardner, I'm most partial to classic "horse operas" like *High Noon* and *Shane*. And, naturally, I have a taste for spaghetti westerns (served with meatballs and plenty of parmesan cheese!).

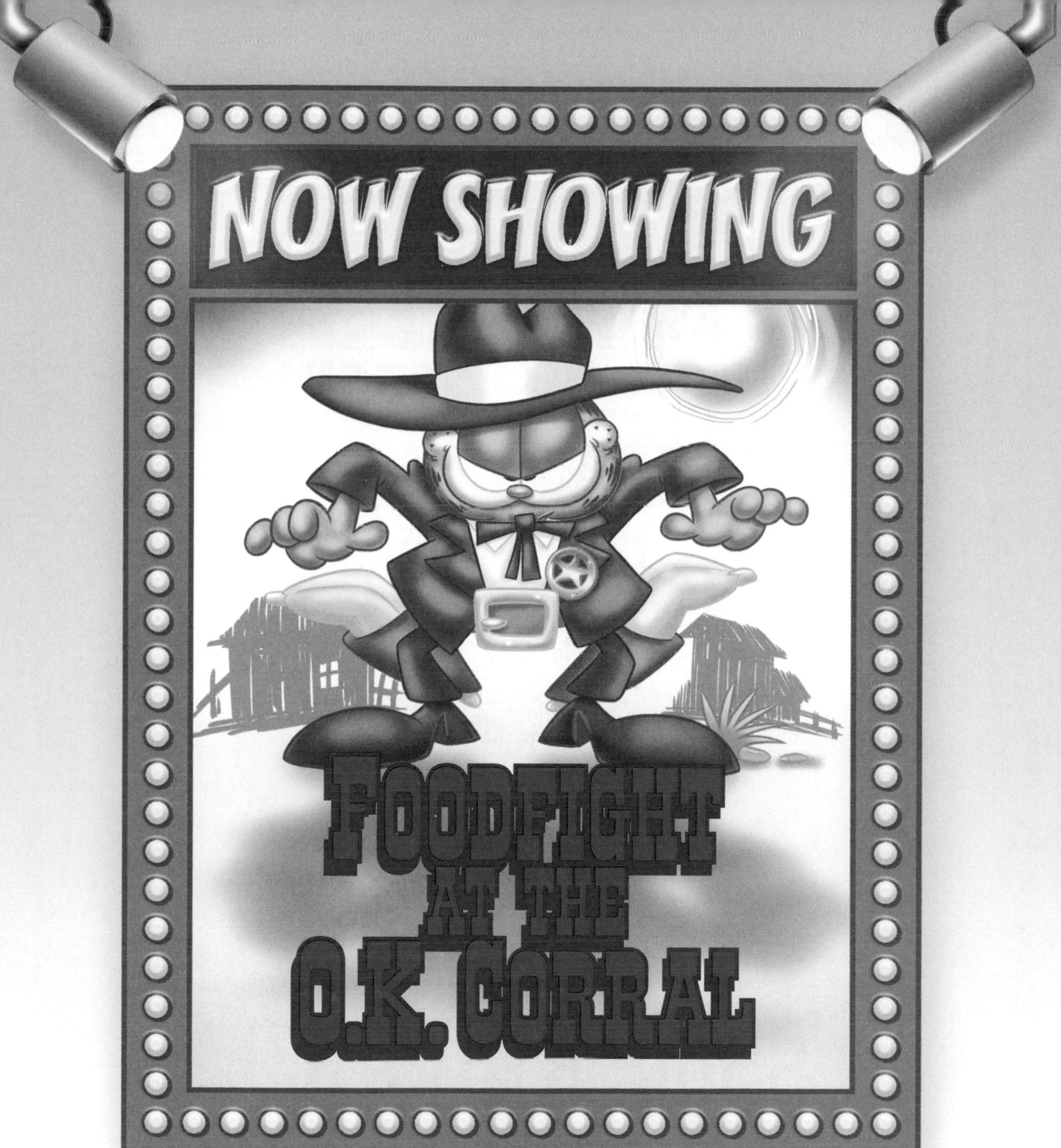
NOW SHOWING
FOODFIGHT
AT THE
O.K. CORRAL

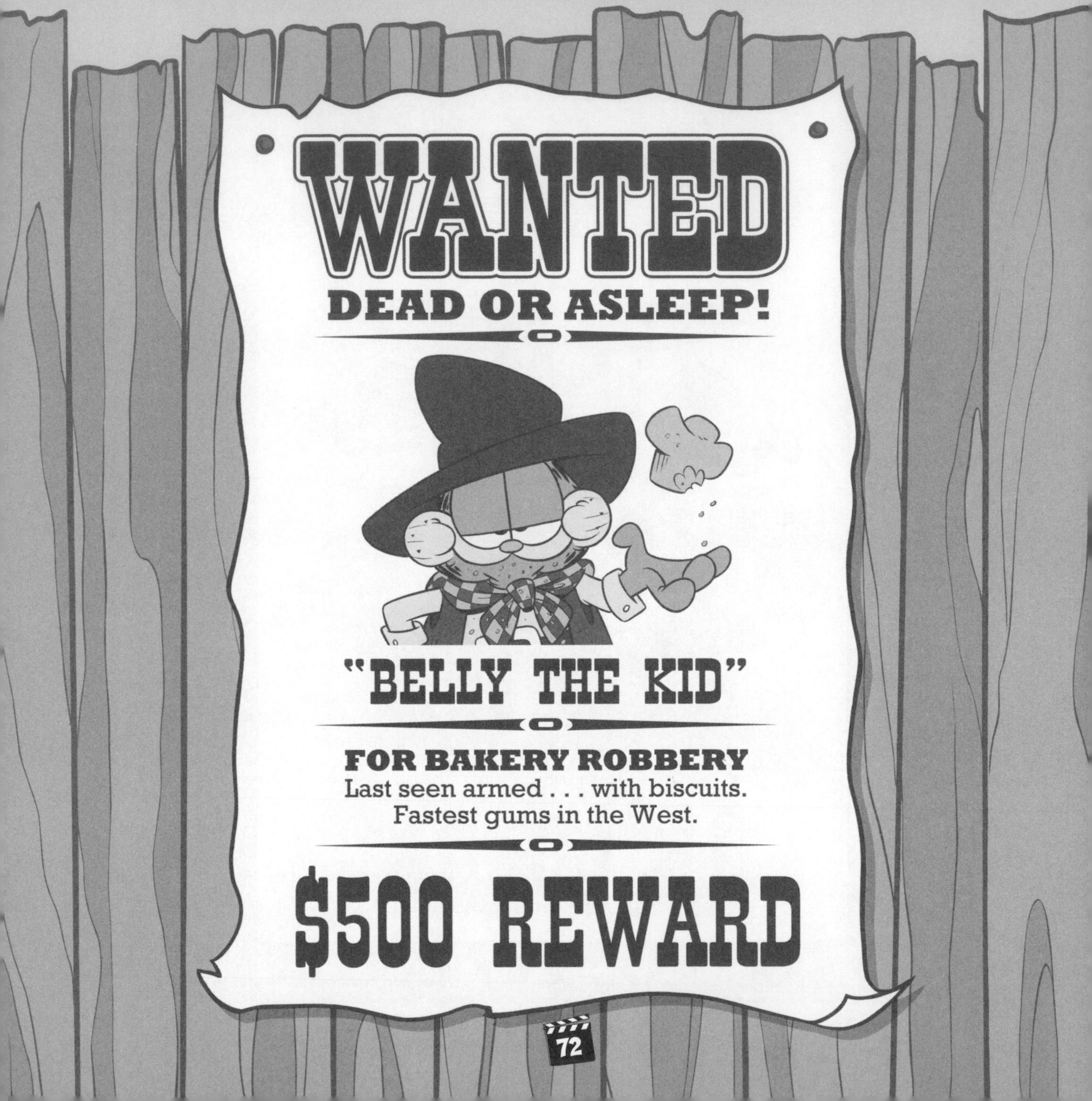
WANTED
DEAD OR ASLEEP!
"BELLY THE KID"
FOR BAKERY ROBBERY
Last seen armed . . . with biscuits.
Fastest gums in the West.
$500 REWARD

SNACK PREVIEWS
FEATURED FLICK

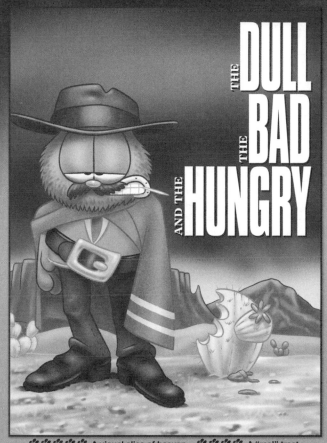

THE DULL, THE BAD AND THE HUNGRY

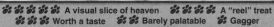

A visual slice of heaven   A "reel" treat
Worth a taste   Barely palatable   Gagger

THE GOOD:
Stylistic spaghetti western spiced
with memorable musical score.

THE BAD:
The movie's pace needs
to giddyup.

THE SCORE:

**"I yawned, I squinted,
and I burped."**

X-RATED

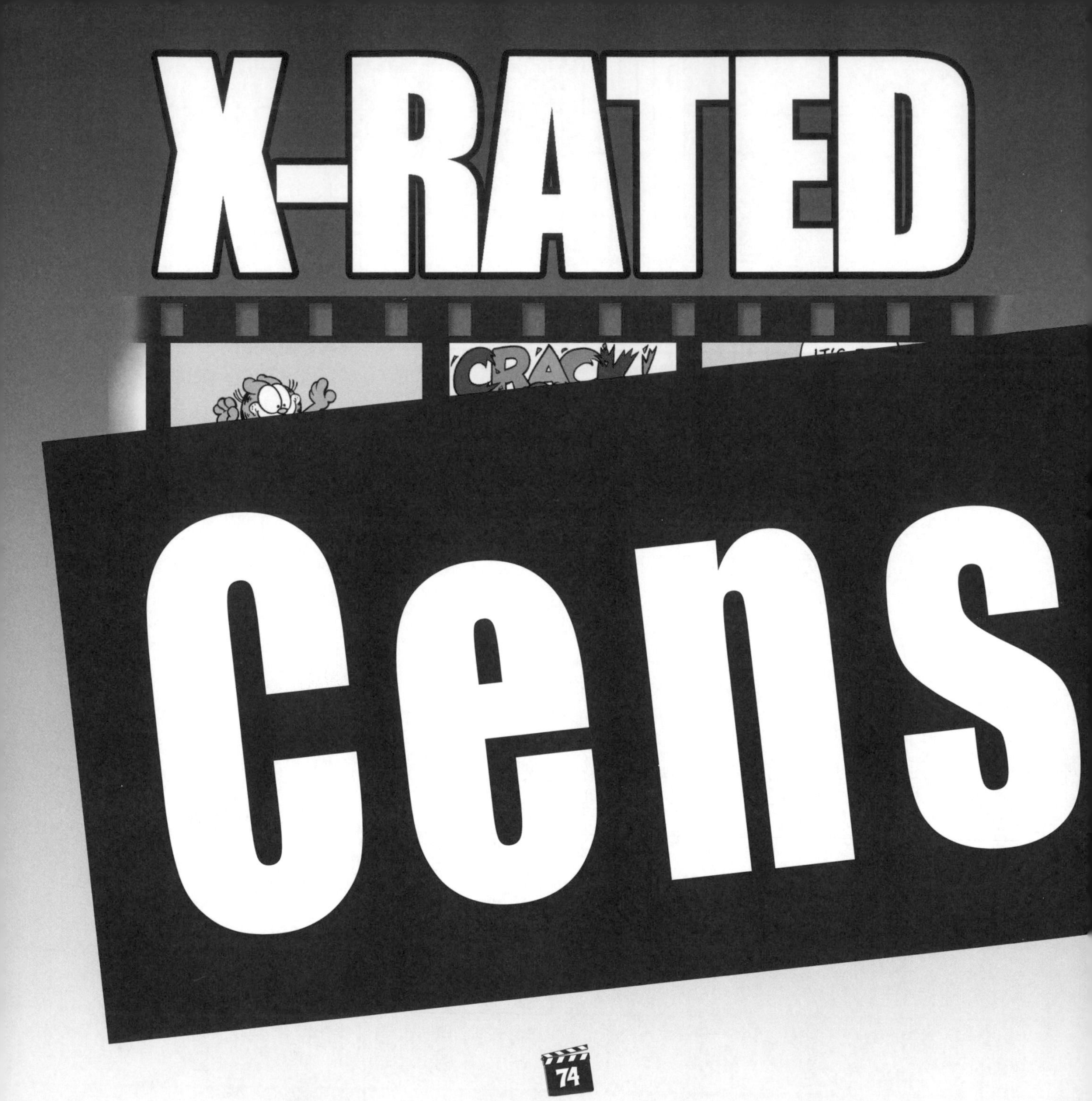
CRACK!

Cens

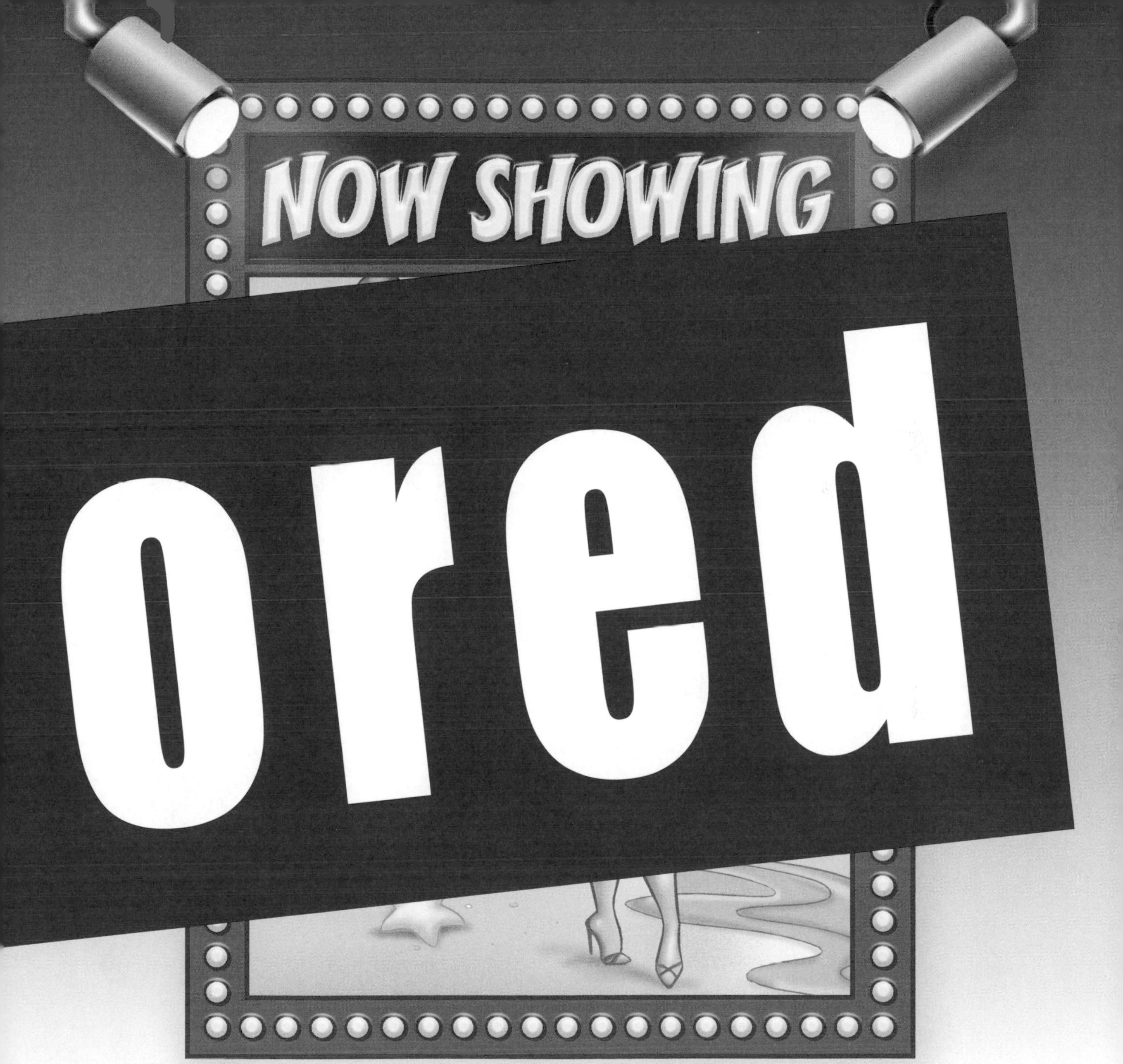
NOW SHOWING
ored

WHEN GENRES COLLIDE!

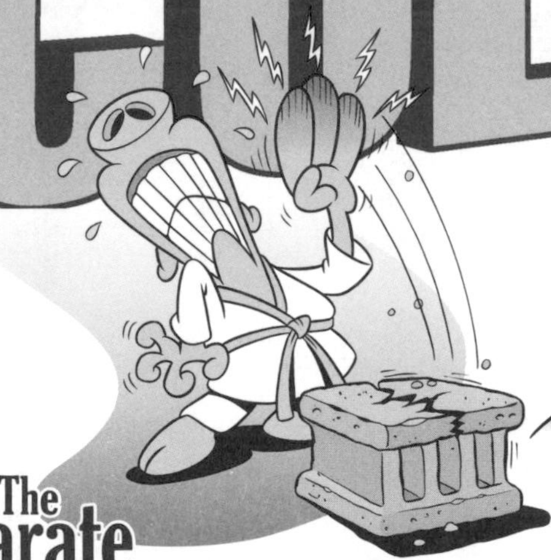

The Karate Pig

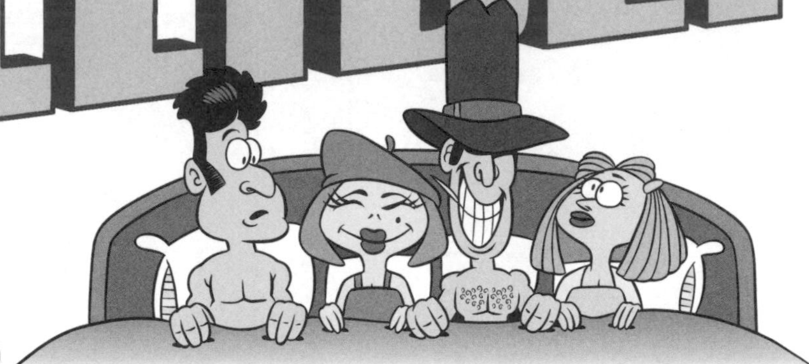

BONNIE & CLYDE & TED & ALICE

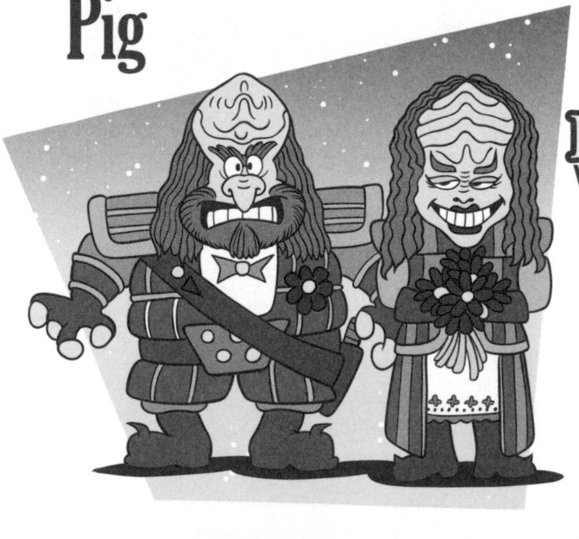

MY BIG FAT KLINGON WEDDING

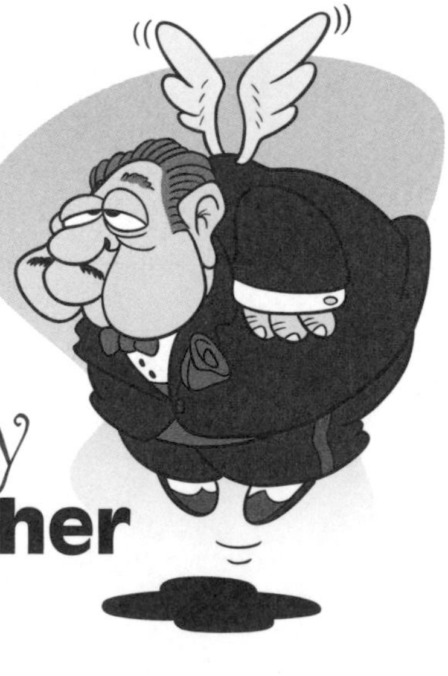

The Fairy Godfather

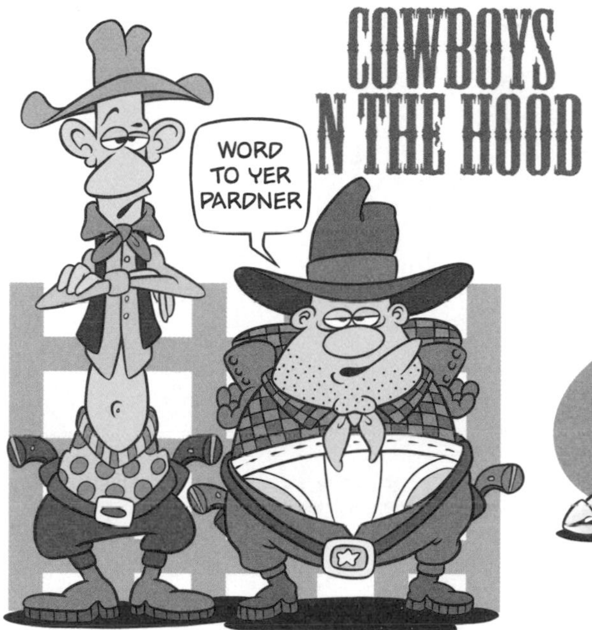
COWBOYS N THE HOOD
WORD TO YER PARDNER

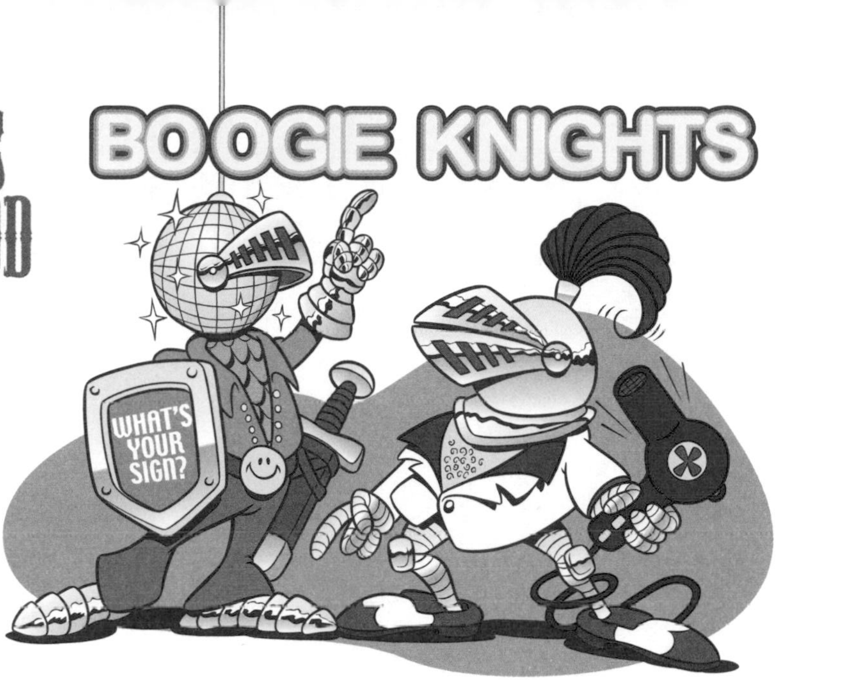
BOOGIE KNIGHTS
WHAT'S YOUR SIGN?

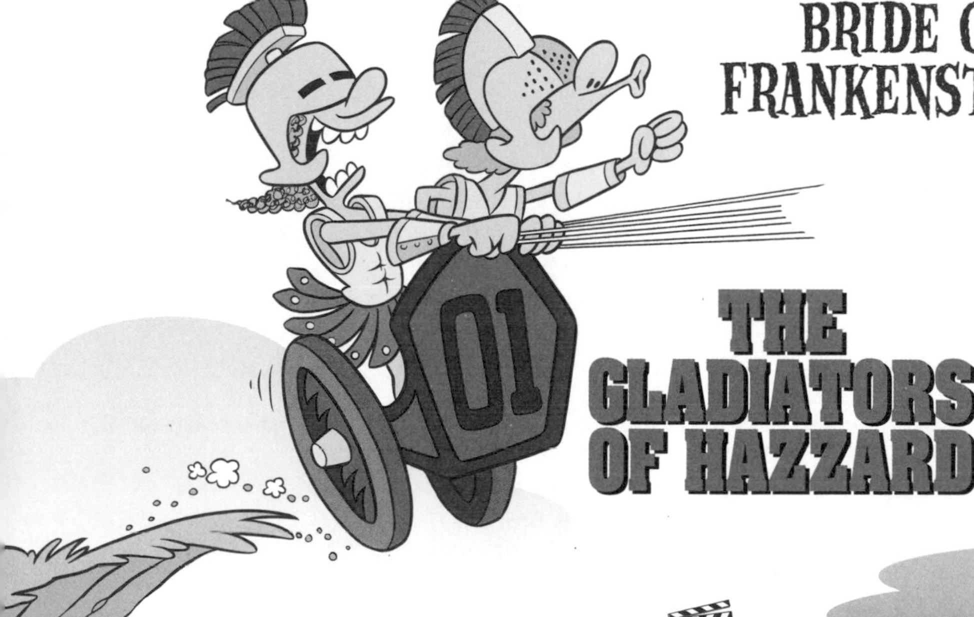
01
THE GLADIATORS OF HAZZARD

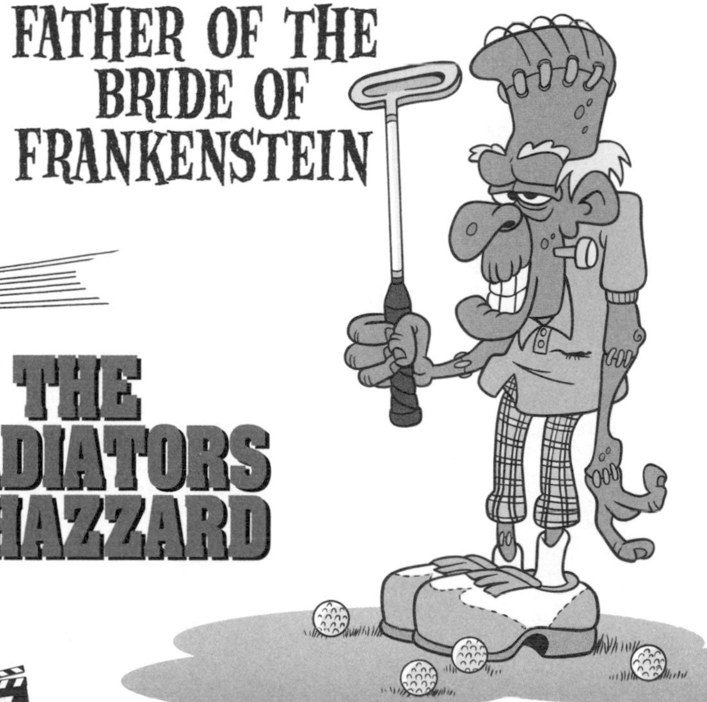
FATHER OF THE BRIDE OF FRANKENSTEIN

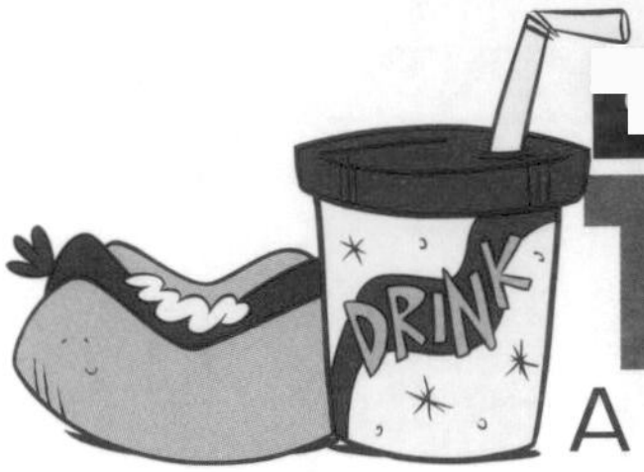
DRINK

MOVIE MADNESS TRIVIA QUIZ

A SILLY SELECTION OF KOOKY QUESTIONS!

1. What's Indiana Jones's day job?

A. Soda jerk
B. Archaeology professor
C. Whip salesman
D. Underwear model

2. The western *The Magnificent Seven* is a remake of which film directed by Akira Kurosawa?

A. *The Seven Sumo*
B. *The Seven Sushi*
C. *The Seven Samurai*
D. *The Seven Year Itch*

3. In *Mary Poppins*, how does the tape measure describe Mary?

A. "Slightly irregular"
B. "Practically perfect in every way"
C. "Bigger than a breadbox"
D. "Va-va-va-va-voom!"

4. What is the name of the leading lady in the musical *Chitty Chitty Bang Bang*?

A. Truly Scrumptious
B. Delightfully Delectable
C. Remarkably Ravenous
D. Prodigiously Fat

5. In *The Wizard of Oz*, where does the wizard live?

A. Hogwarts
B. Gotham City
C. The Emerald City
D. In his mother's basement

6. The line "If you build it, he will come" from *Field of Dreams* refers to what?

A. A chili parlor in Cincinnati
B. A basketball court in the Bronx
C. A baseball diamond in Iowa
D. A donut shop in Rhode Island

7. Who was originally cast as Dr. Zaius in the 1968 version of *Planet of the Apes*?

A. Laurence Olivier
B. Lancelot Link, Secret Chimp
C. Edward G. Robinson
D. Jerry Lewis

8. What was the name of the Indian who liked to smoke in *Dances with Wolves*?

A. Ten Bears
B. Eleven Goats
C. Five Gerbils
D. Two Turtles

9. In 1979's *Alien*, what happens when the crew sits down to a meal?

A. Someone uses the wrong fork
B. Sigourney Weaver drinks too much Tang
C. The shrimp scampi is undercooked
D. An alien bursts out of John Hurt's stomach

10. Which brothers directed the comedy *There's Something About Mary*?

A. Coen Brothers
B. Farrelly Brothers
C. Smothers Brothers
D. Doobie Brothers

11. **What was the rodent's name in the classic animated film *Dumbo*?**

A. Ratso Rizzo

B. Socrates

C. Timothy Q. Mouse

D. Topo Gigio

12. **What incident causes Roman governor Messala to send his former friend Ben-Hur to a slave galley?**

A. A flatulent horse

B. A falling brick

C. An incontinent camel

D. A burp of Biblical proportions

13. **What was actor/director Erich von Stroheim famous for wearing?**

A. A thong

B. A monocle

C. A truss

D. Gloria Swanson's nightgown

14. **What is the English name of the Chinese film *Wo Hu Cang Long*, directed by Ang Lee?**

A. *Snoozing Rooster, Hidden Boll Weevil*

B. *Drooling Donkey, Hammered Monkey*

C. *Squatting Buffalo, Hungry Dung Beetle*

D. *Crouching Tiger, Hidden Dragon*

15. **What is the name of the film in which Billy Crystal and Meg Ryan fall in love?**

A. *When a Man Loves a Woman*

B. *When Harry Met Sally*

C. *When Rand Met McNally*

D. *When Larry Hit Curly*

16. **What is the name of the character Al Pacino played in *Scarface*?**

A. Tony Roma

B. Tony Montana

C. Tony Danza

D. Tony the Tiger

17. **Which of these film luminaries never won an Oscar® for Best Director?**

A. Hitchcock, Altman, Scorsese

B. Kubrick, Sturges, Welles

C. Spanky, Alfalfa, Buckwheat

D. All of the above

18. **Which of the following is NOT a real horror movie title?**

A. *Jesse James Meets Frankenstein's Daughter*

B. *Frankenstein General Hospital*

C. *Shaun of the Dead*

D. *Dr. Terror's House of Pancakes*

19. **Which of these American cities is NOT the name of an acclaimed film?**

A. Philadelphia

B. Fargo

C. Frostbite Falls

D. Chicago

20. **Which movie was number one on the American Film Institute's list of the top 100 American films of the last 100 years?**

A. *Smokey and the Bandit*

B. *Plan 9 from Outer Space*

C. *Joe Dirt*

D. *Citizen Kane*

ANSWERS 1.B 2.C 3.B 4.A 5.C 6.C 7.C 8.A 9.D 10.B 11.C 12.B 13.B 14.D 15.B 16.B 17.D 18.D 19.C 20.D

OUTRAGEOUS OUTTAKES

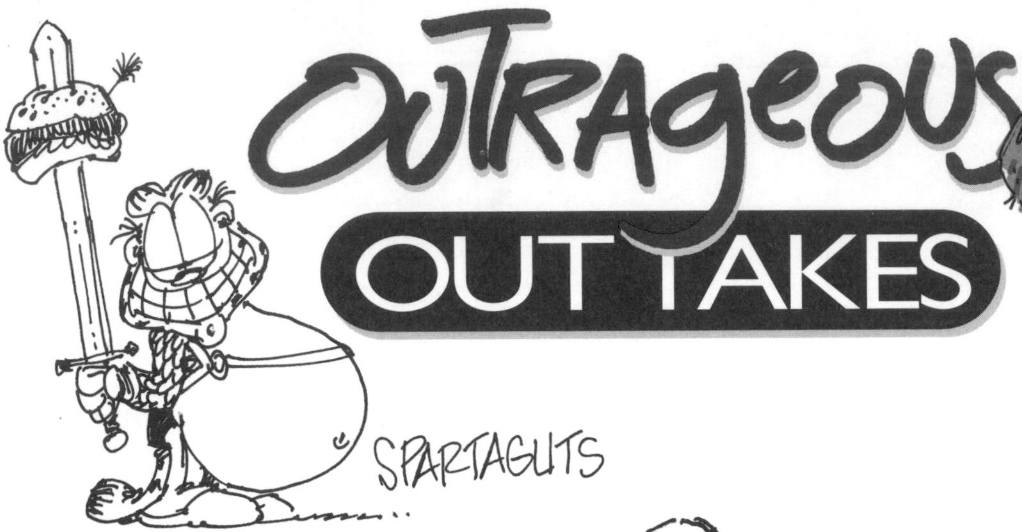

SPARTAGUTS

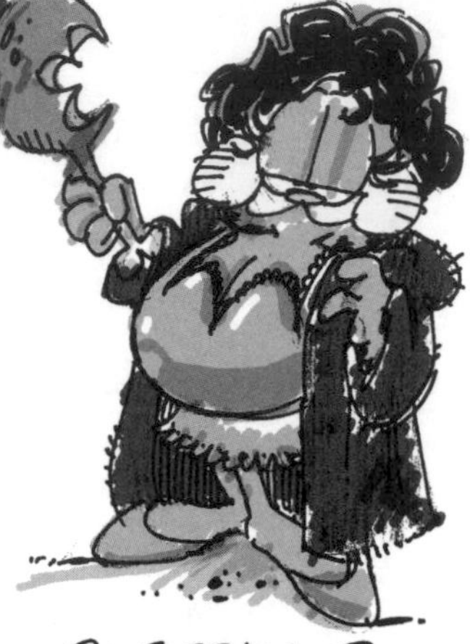

BUTTERBALL 8

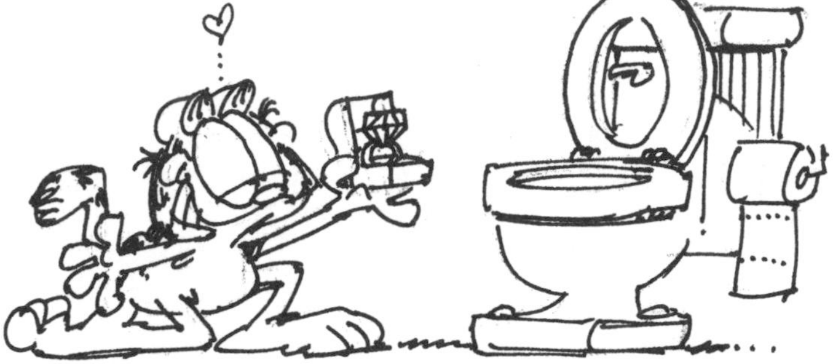

ROMANCING THE THRONE

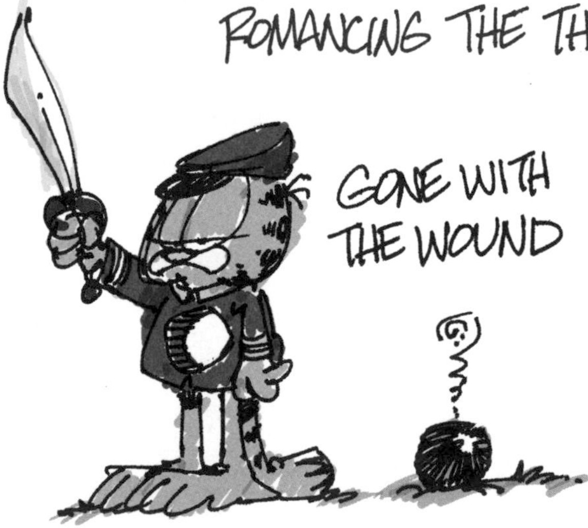

GONE WITH THE WOUND

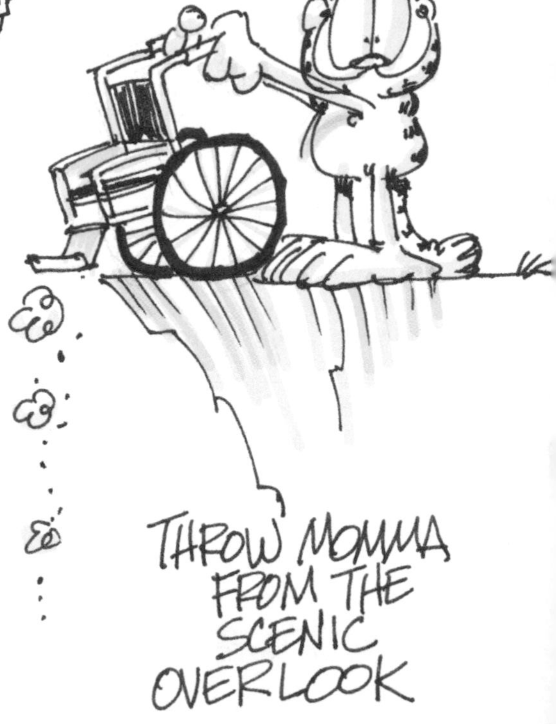

THROW MOMMA FROM THE SCENIC OVERLOOK

BLING BLADE

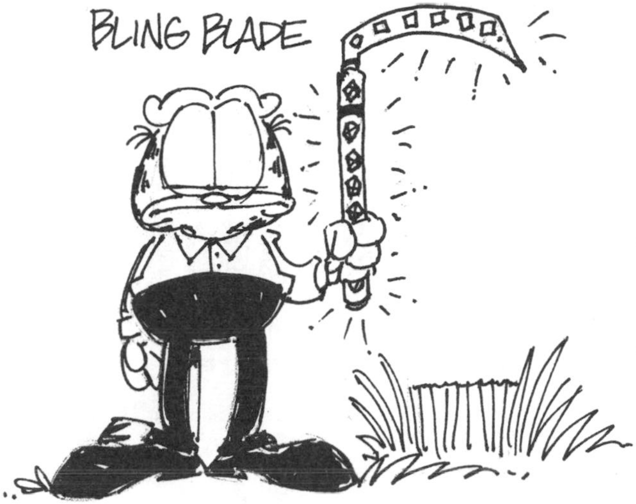

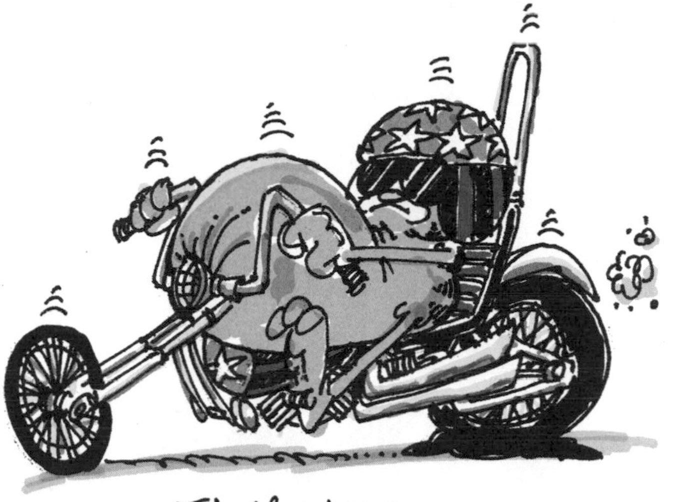

EASY WIDER

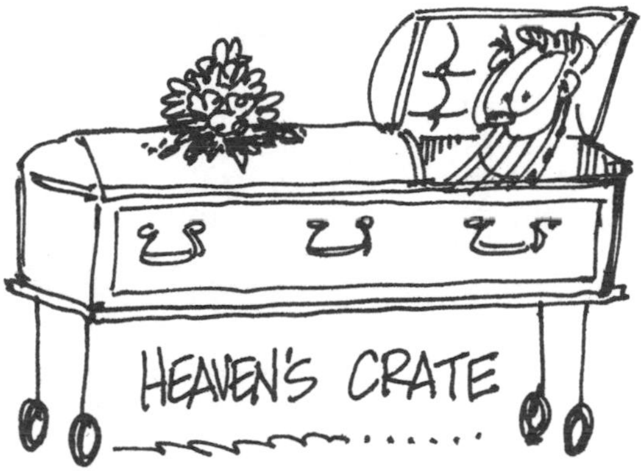

HEAVEN'S CRATE

FROM HERE TO PATERNITY

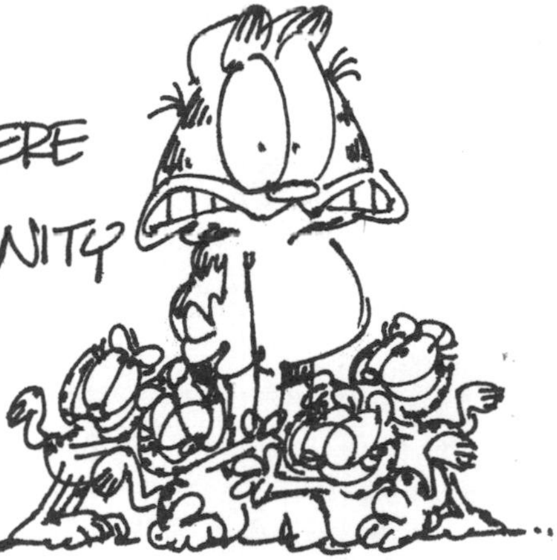

DUDE, WHERE'S MY FUR?

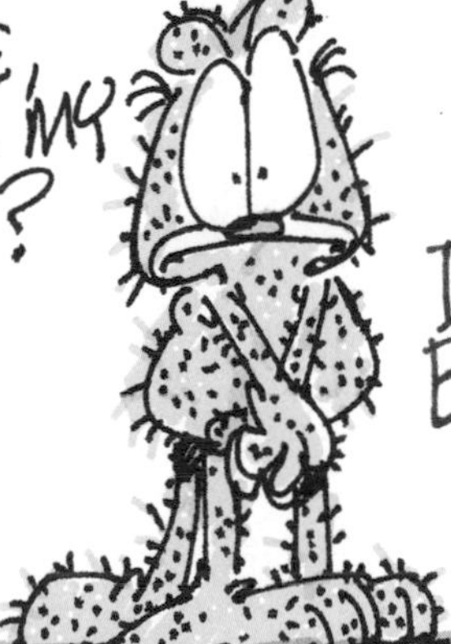

DEEP BLOAT

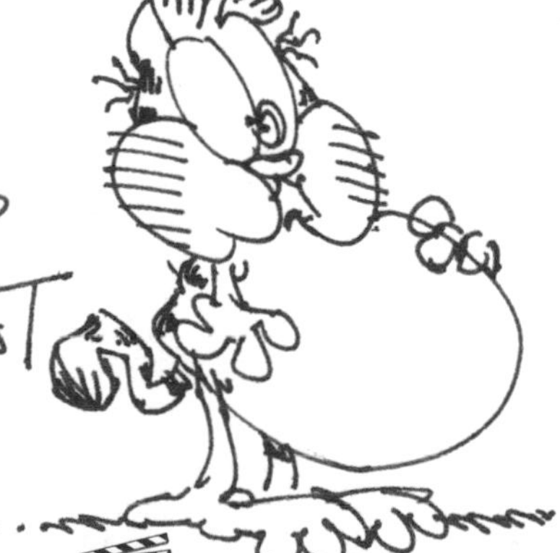

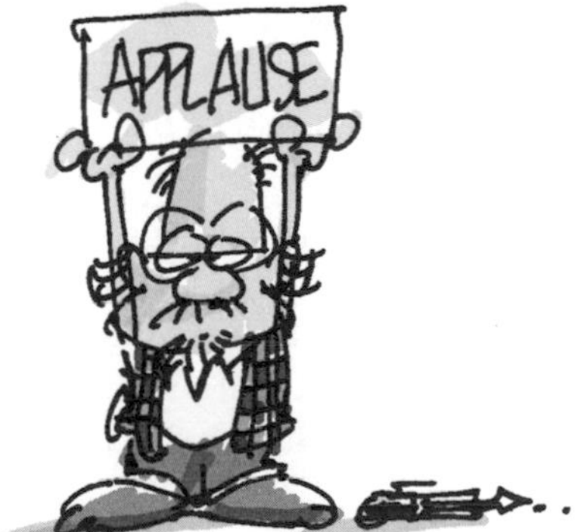
APPLAUSE

GARFIELD
A TALE OF TWO MOVIES

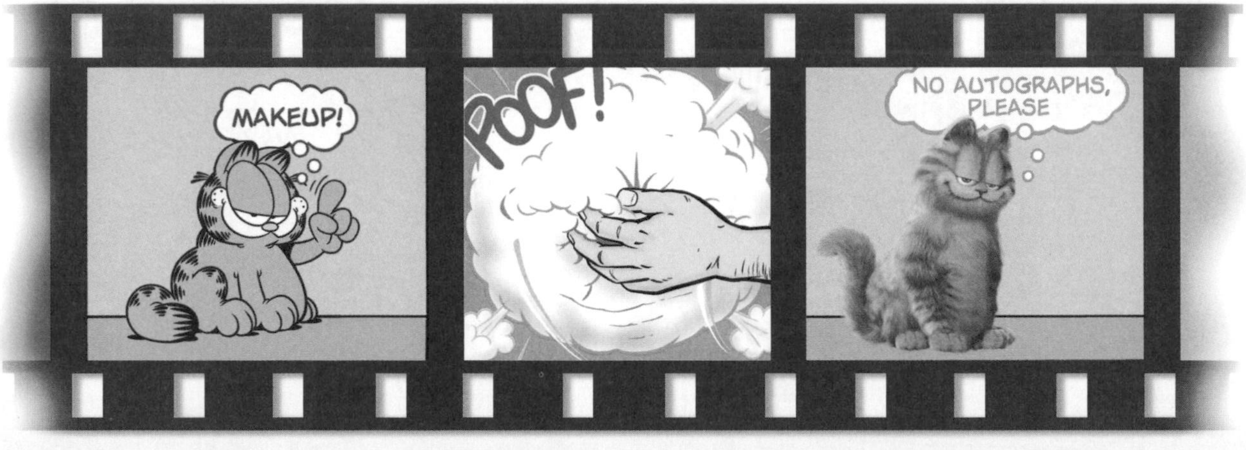
MAKEUP!
POOF!
NO AUTOGRAPHS, PLEASE

You can consider the previous eighty-one pages of this book Coming Attractions. Now it's time for the Feature Presentation: ME. I'm a bonafide movie star with two—count 'em, two—feature films under my big fat furry belt. (Hey, I put the "wide" in "wide-screen"!)

After conquering comic strips, books, and TV, I was ready to sink my teeth into the movies. The biggest problem was keeping enough lasagna on the set!

I don't want to brag, but I turned in quite a well-rounded performance, if I do say so myself. I had the emotional intensity of Robert De Niro, the eloquence of Laurence Olivier, and the hunky good looks of Brad Pitt. I can't believe the Oscars snubbed me. Envy: It's the curse of all great actors.

Don't get me wrong. I love being a media darling: the glitz, the glamour, the parties, the adoring fans. The only downside is the pesky paparazzi who try to get shots of me in the litter box!

In this section, you'll see highlights from my first movie and get a sneak peek at the sensational sequel, *Garfield's A Tail of Two Kitties*, in which I play two roles (because too much of me is never enough!). So read on . . . and enjoy!

ife couldn't be sweeter for Garfield. Parked on a comfortable overstuffed chair in front of the TV, feasting on his favorite dish—lasagna—he's the master of his universe. That is until his owner, Jon, takes in sweet-but-dimwitted pooch Odie, turning Garfield's perfect world upside down. Now Garfield wants only one thing: Odic out of his home and life!

But when the hapless pup disappears, Garfield, maybe for the first time in his life, feels responsible. With an uncharacteristic amount of energy and courage, Garfield manages to pull himself away from the TV and spring into action. He's on a mission to save Odie . . . and get back to his beloved chair!

GARFIELD
THE MOVIE

Garfield director Peter Hewitt confers on the set with Jim Davis.

A STAR IS BORN!

Jennifer Love Hewitt (Liz the vet) cuddles with her chubby costar.

GARFIELD THE MOVIE

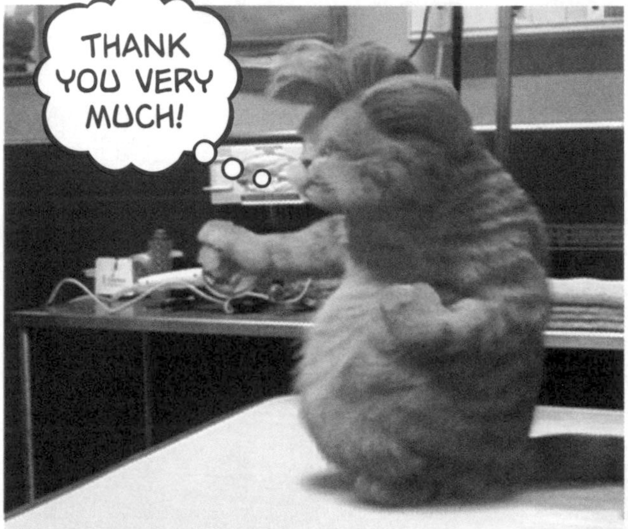
THANK YOU VERY MUCH!

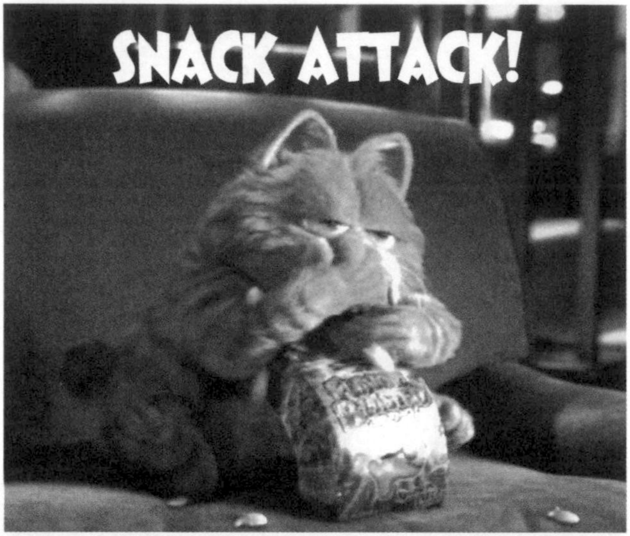
SNACK ATTACK!

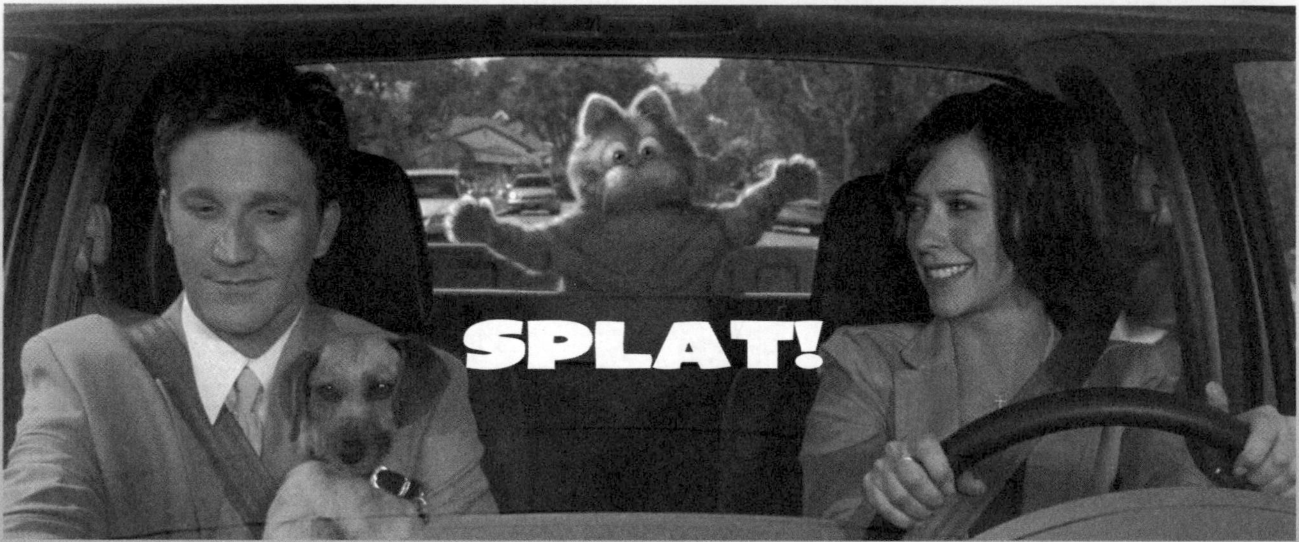
SPLAT!

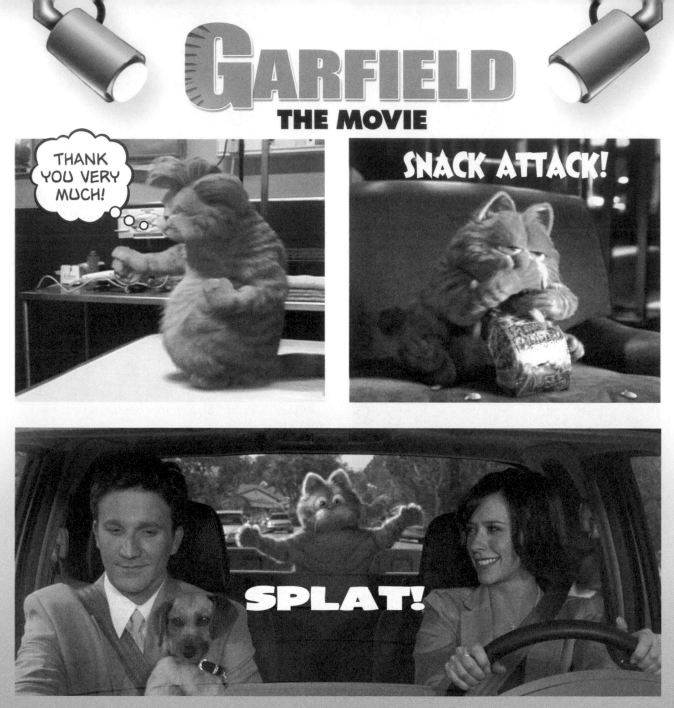

GARFIELD THE MOVIE

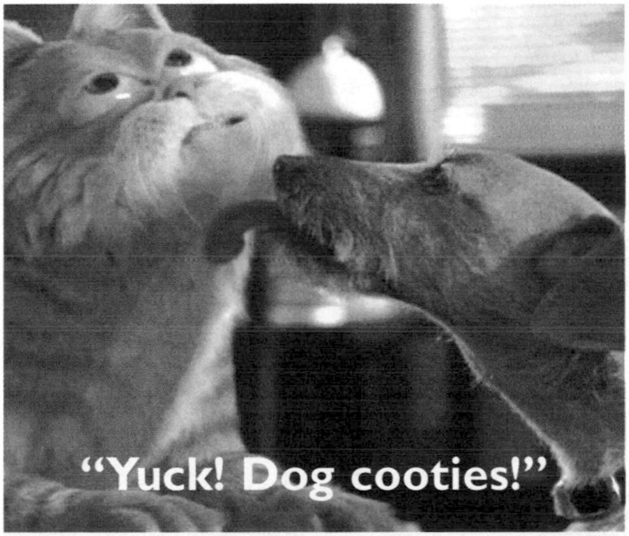
"Yuck! Dog cooties!"

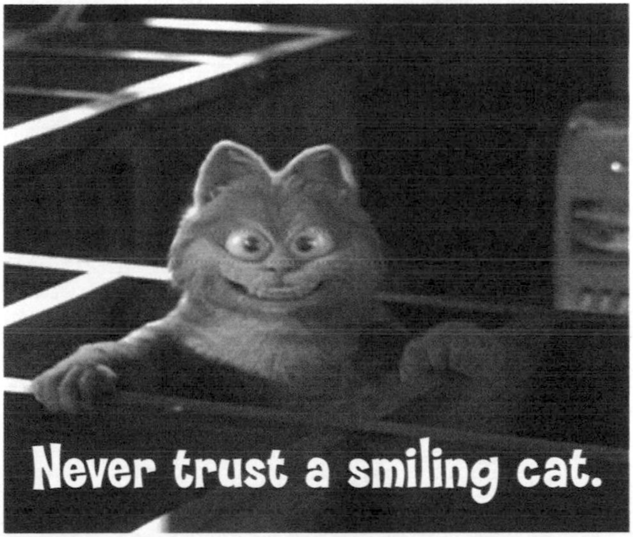
Never trust a smiling cat.

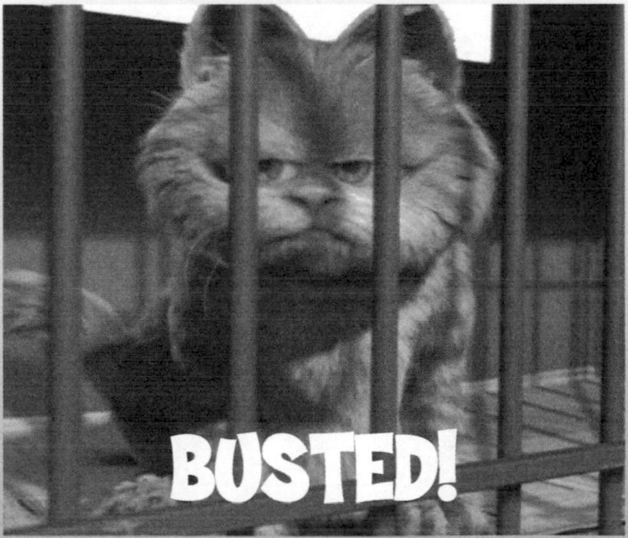
BUSTED!

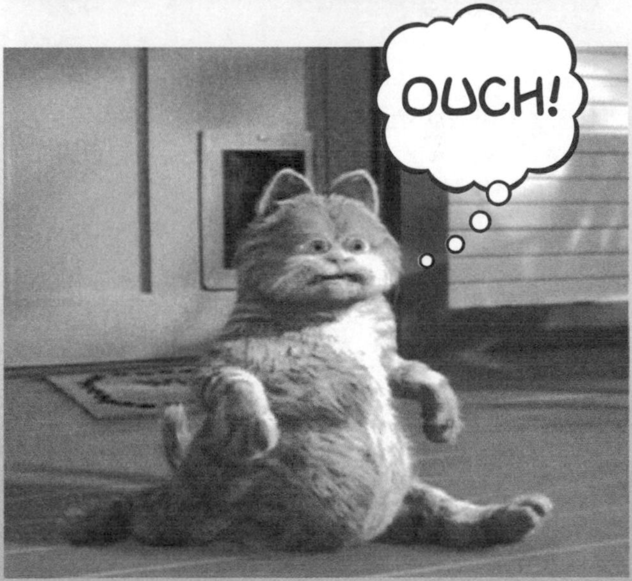
OUCH!

GARFIELD'S
A TAIL OF TWO KITTIES

THE CAST

Garfield as himself

Prince XII, Garfield's royal
look-alike

Odie, Garfield's dopey
doggie pal

Jennifer Love Hewitt
as Dr. Liz Wilson

Breckin Meyer
as Jon Arbuckle

Billy Connolly as
nasty Lord Dargis

86

In his all-new movie adventure, Garfield follows his owner, Jon, to England—the land of the royals—where Garfield is mistaken for a noble cat who has inherited a castle. Garfield savors the royal treatment afforded by his loyal subjects, including an eager-to-please butler, a (very) English bulldog, a duck, a hare, a goose, a bull, a ferret, a pig—and a Shakespeare-quoting mouse. However, Garfield's reign is in jeopardy. The nefarious Lord Dargis is determined to do away with Garfield so he can turn the castle into a resort. Meanwhile, Garfield's royal double, Prince XII—the castle's true master—has surfaced and made his way back home.

Garfield and Prince, along with faithful pooch Odie and the castle's menagerie, join forces to save the castle and thwart Dargis's plans.

The original cast of *Garfield* is back for the sequel, which is in the capable hands of director Tim Hill.

Rhythm & Hues is also back on board to handle the special effects and keep Garfield looking good for his second big-screen appearance.

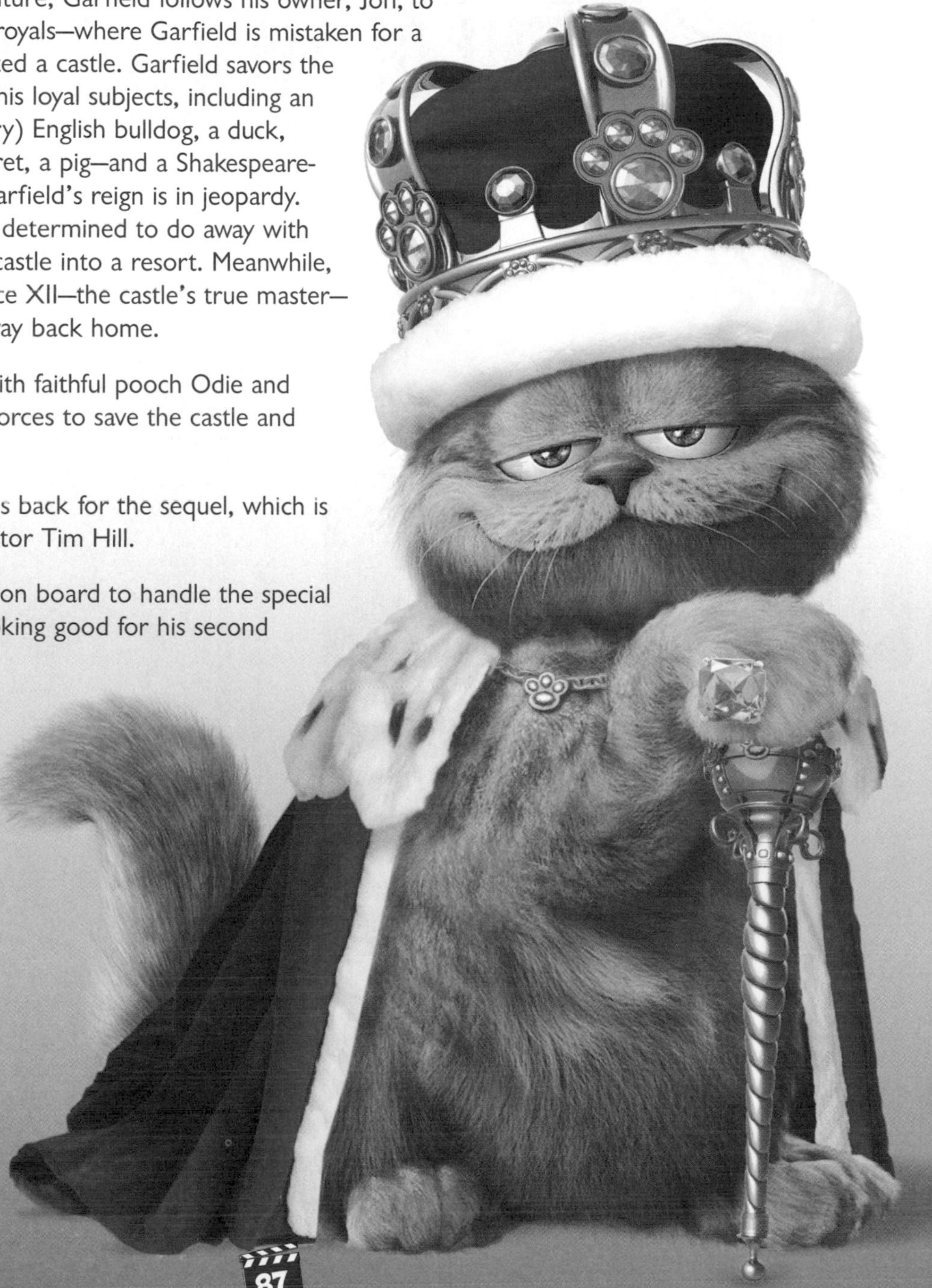

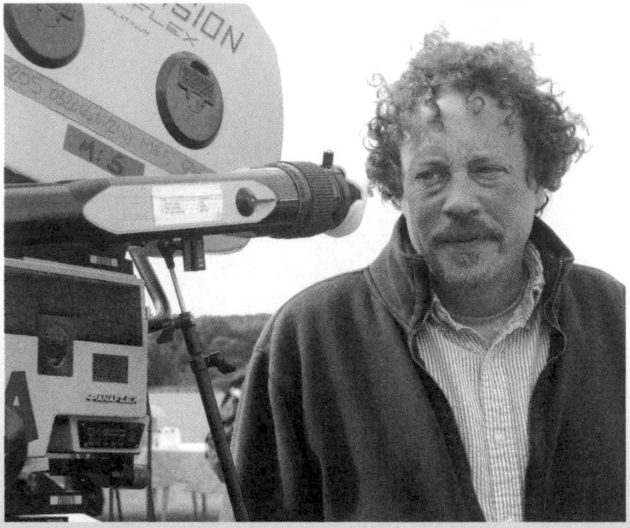

Left: Director Tim Hill sizes up a shot. Tim's Hollywood résumé includes directorial duties on **Muppets from Space** *and* **Max Keeble's Big Move,** *and writing for* **The SpongeBob SquarePants Movie.**

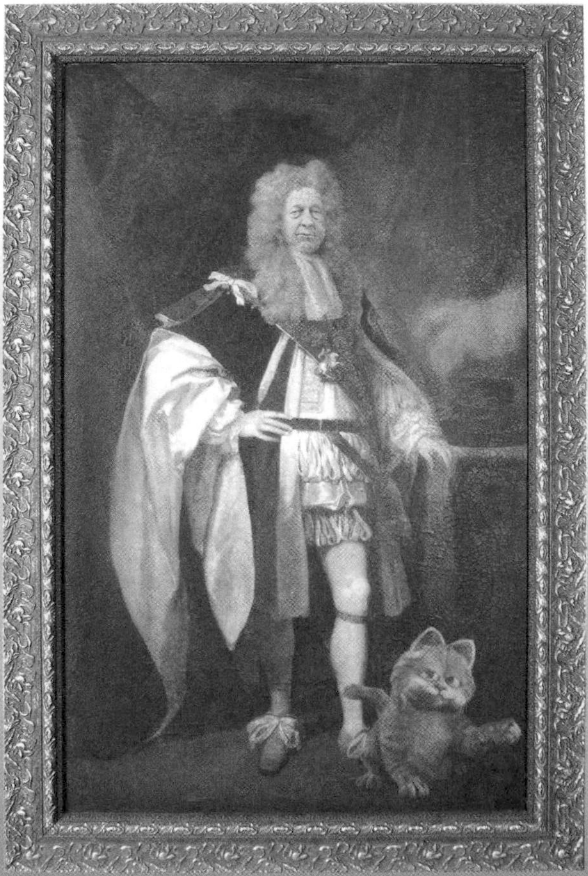

Garfield creator Jim Davis makes a special cameo "appearance" in a painting of one of Prince XII's ancestors. Check out that awesome head of hair!

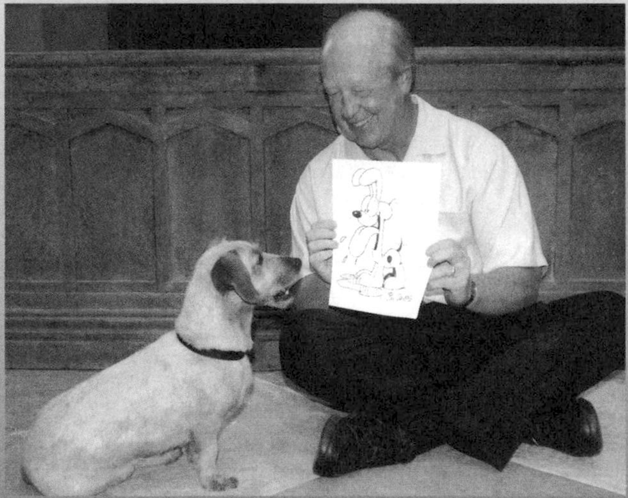

Odie meets his cartoon counterpart.

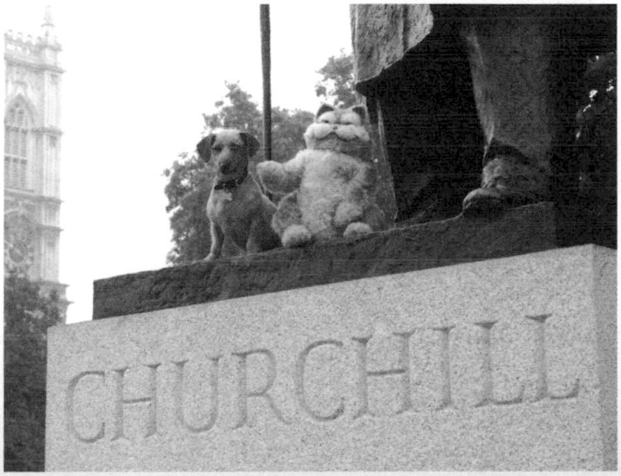
CHURCHILL

G2 features a veritable travelogue of famous British landmarks.

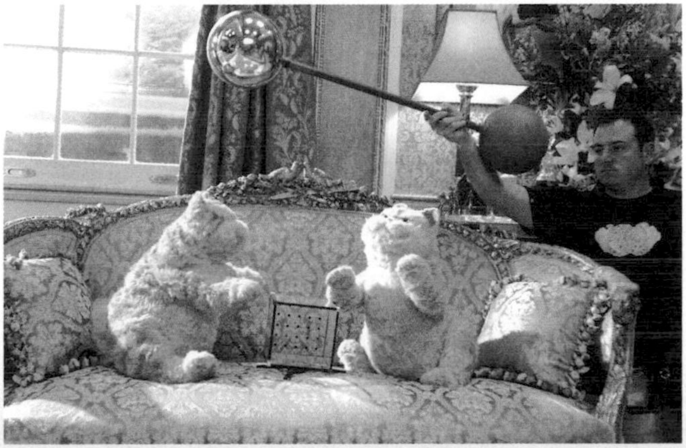

As in the first Garfield movie, stuffed stand-ins were used during principal photography. These were replaced with computer-generated characters for the final film.

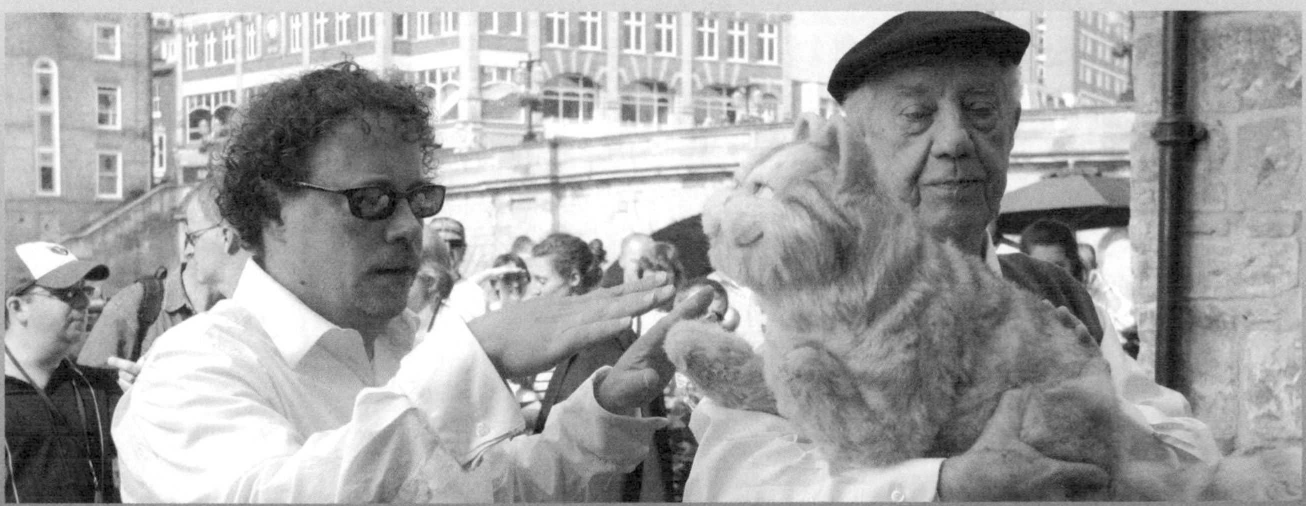

Director Tim Hill works out a scene with actor Ian Abercrombie (Smithee) and friend.

GARFIELD'S
A TAIL OF TWO KITTIES

The movie poster features a double dose of the famous fat cat.

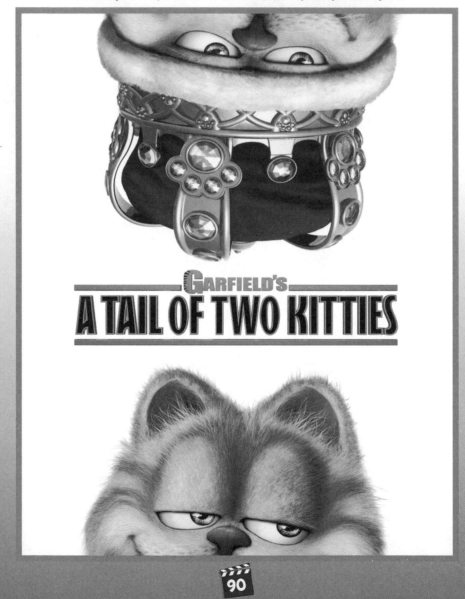

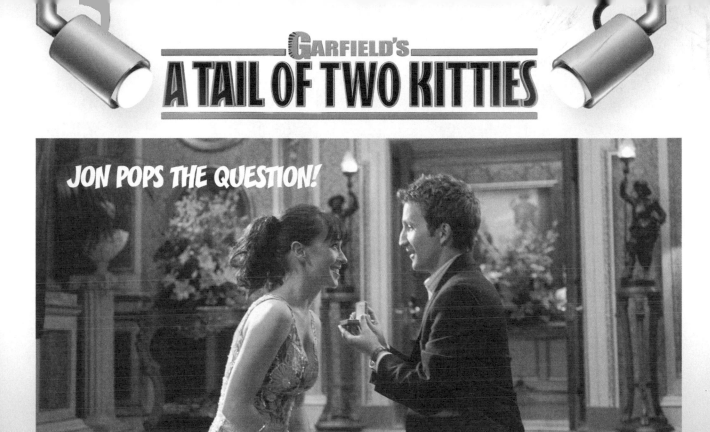

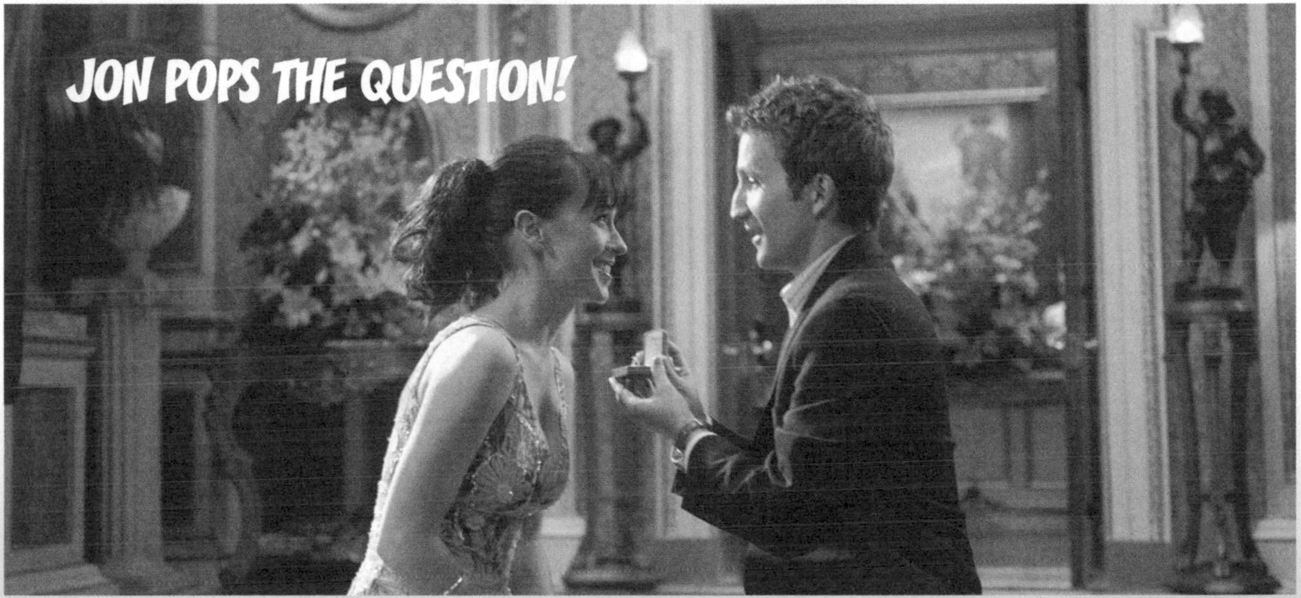
JON POPS THE QUESTION!

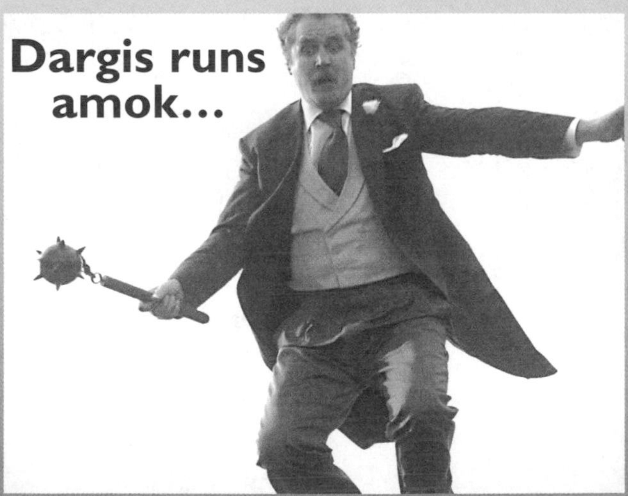
Dargis runs amok...

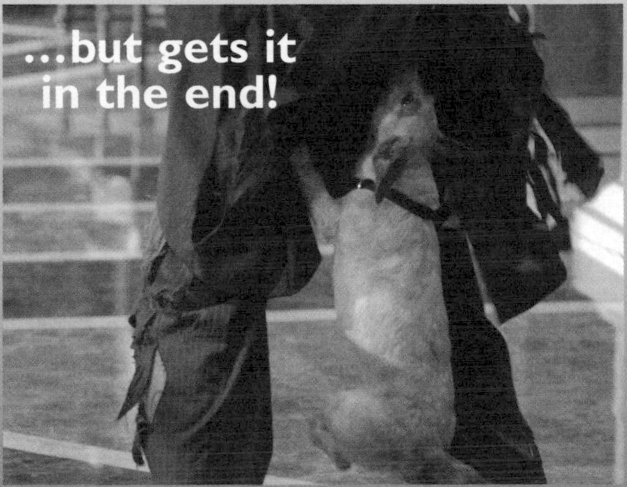
...but gets it in the end!

ANIMAL ANTICS

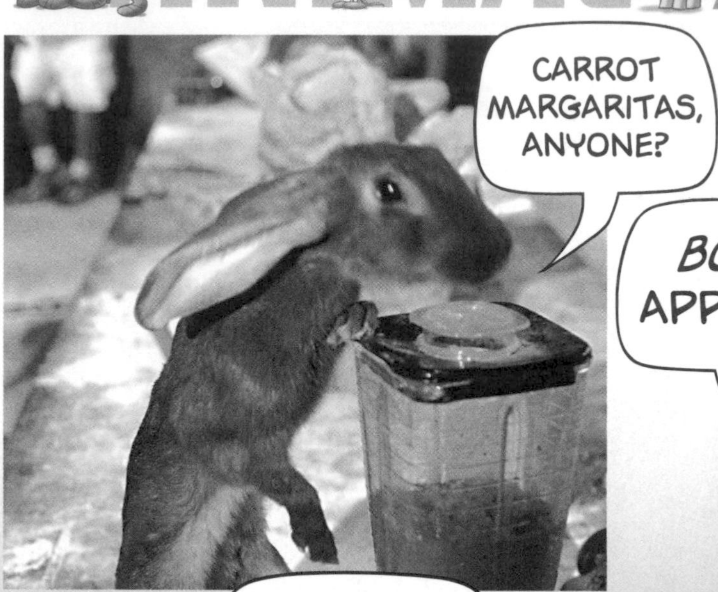
CARROT MARGARITAS, ANYONE?

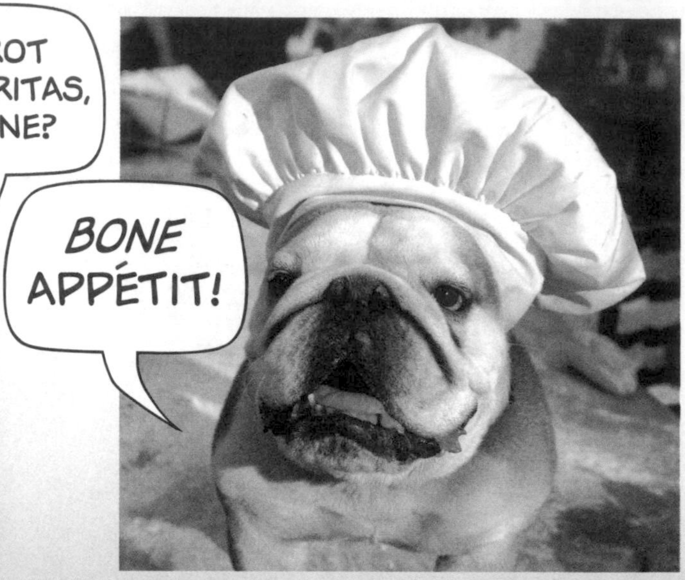
BONE APPÉTIT!

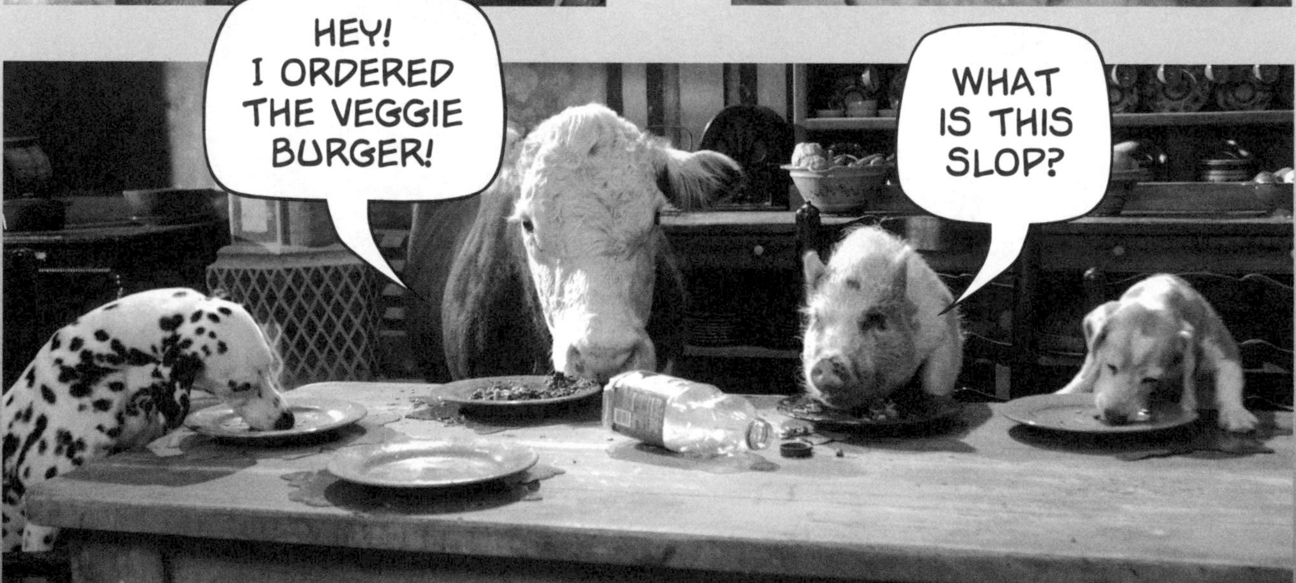
HEY! I ORDERED THE VEGGIE BURGER!
WHAT IS THIS SLOP?

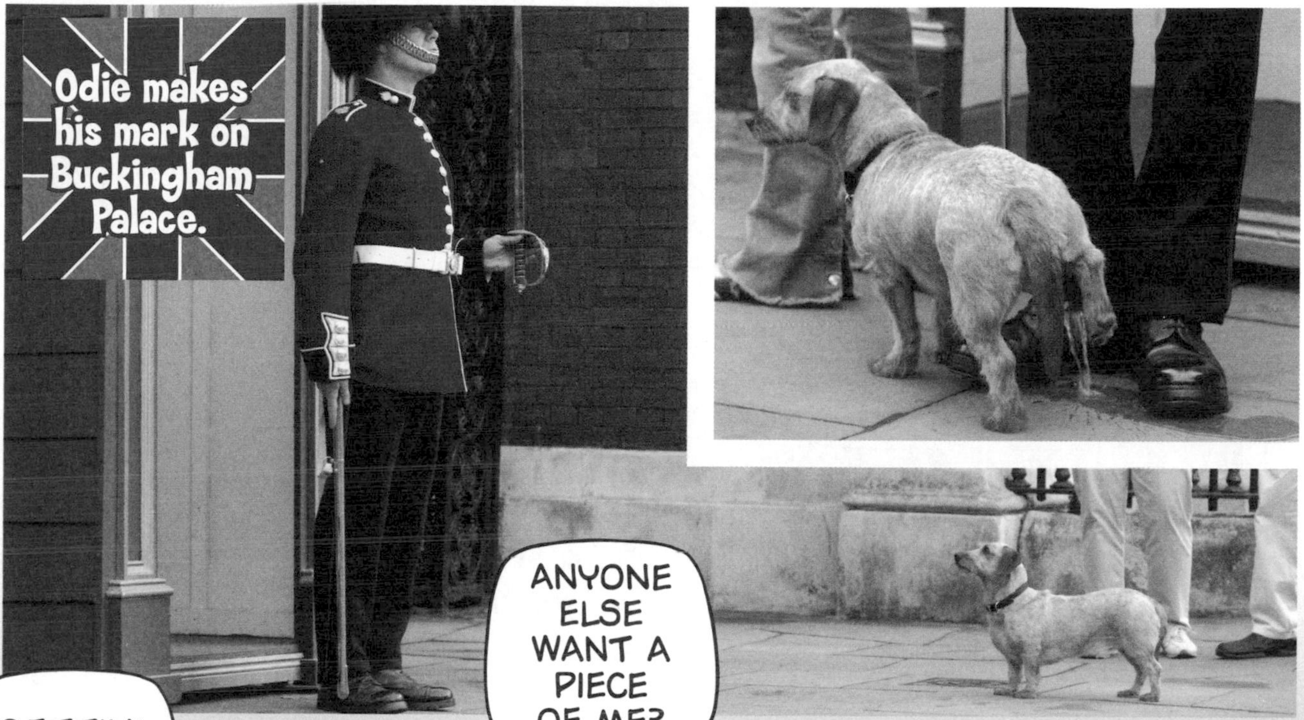
Odie makes his mark on Buckingham Palace.

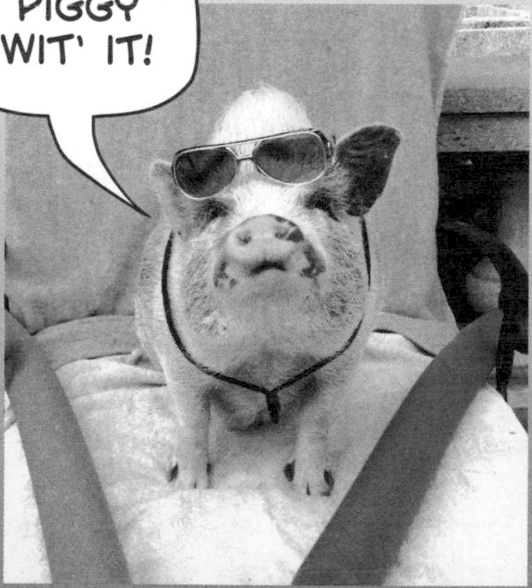
GETTIN' PIGGY WIT' IT!

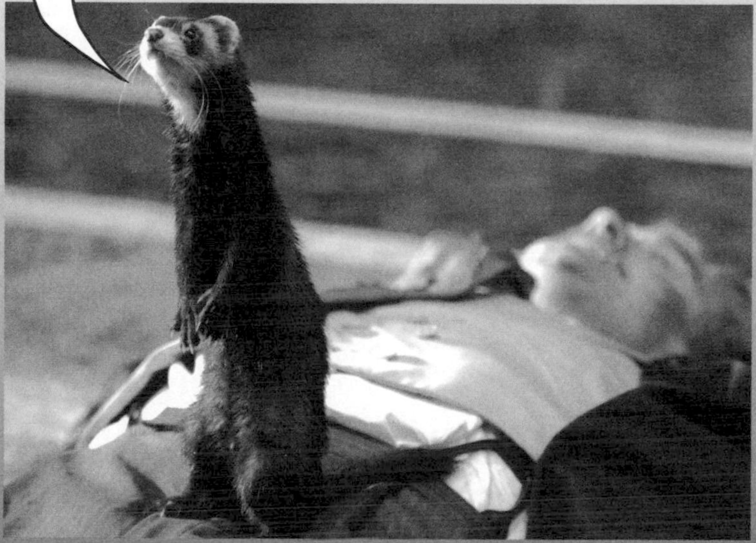
ANYONE ELSE WANT A PIECE OF ME?

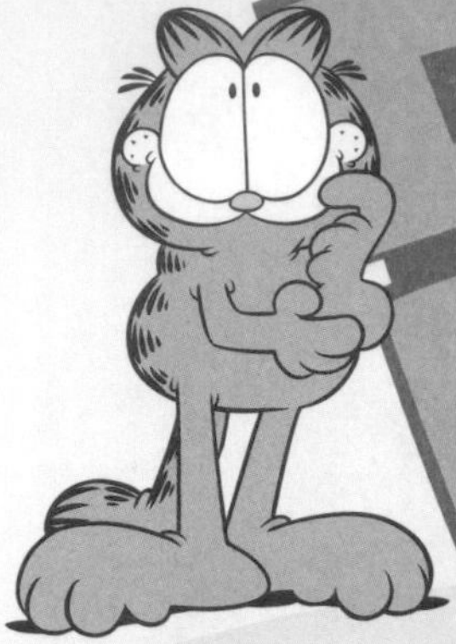

DID YOU KNOW?

Jennifer Love Hewitt was listed at number 32 on the *Maxim* magazine "Hot 100 of 2005" list.

There are approximately 400 computer-generated shots of Garfield in *Garfield: The Movie.*

Breckin Meyer is actually allergic to cats!

Ian Abercrombie (Smithee) had a recurring role on TV's *Seinfeld.*

Odie is actually played by twin dogs: brother and sister Tyler and Chloe.

John Davis (no relation to Garfield creator Jim Davis) has produced more than seventy films, including *Predator, Grumpy Old Men, Dr. Dolittle*, and *I, Robot.*

Tim Hill is the nephew of director George Roy Hill, whose films include *The Sting, Butch Cassidy and the Sundance Kid*, and *The World According to Garp.*

Billy Connolly (Dargis) played Uncle Monty in the film version of *Lemony Snicket's A Series of Unfortunate Events.*

Jim Davis's favorite movie is *Airplane* ("Love those fighting Girl Scouts!")

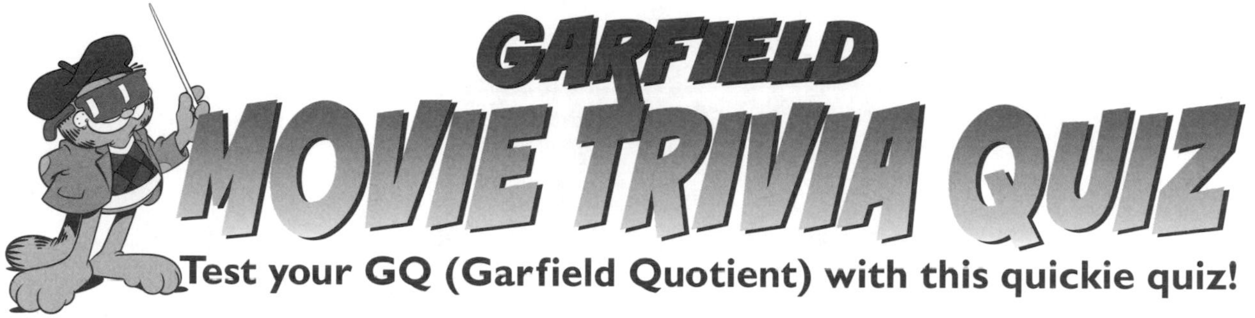

GARFIELD MOVIE TRIVIA QUIZ

Test your GQ (Garfield Quotient) with this quickie quiz!

1. Whose *Garfield: The Movie* cameo appearance ended up on the cutting-room floor?

A. Orson the Pig
B. Snoop Dogg
C. Paris Hilton
D. Jim Davis

2. What was the villain's name in the first Garfield movie?

A. Smiley Chapstick
B. Giggly Chipmunk
C. Happy Chapman
D. Victor Von Doom

3. In the first movie, what does Odie wear during his TV debut?

A. An eye patch
B. A disco suit
C. An "I hate cats" sweater
D. Lederhosen

4. Which animal appears in *Garfield's A Tail of Two Kitties?*

A. Ian the Rabid Raccoon
B. McBunny
C. Colin Cockatiel
D. Helmut the Schizoid Schnauzer

5. Why is Dr. Liz Wilson in England?

A. To give a speech at the Royal Animal Conservancy
B. To perform an emergency flea dip on the queen's corgi
C. Snagged the lead in the London revival of *Cats*
D. She has a really bad craving for fish and chips

6. What does Lord Dargis want to do with Carlyle Castle?

A. Auction it off on eBay
B. Turn it into a resort
C. Turn it into a White Castle
D. Redecorate it with black velvet paintings

ANSWERS: 1. D 2. C 3. D 4. B 5. A 6. B

A QUARTET OF GARFIELD CLASSICS

ODIE UNLEASHED! Garfield Lets the Dog Out

After years of living in Garfield's supersized shadow, Odie finally breaks loose with a book of his own!

0-345-46464-8 • 8" x 8" • 128 pages
$12.95 / $17.95 CAN • Ballantine Trade Paperback

GARFIELD'S GUIDE TO EVERYTHING

The fat cat weighs in with his not-so-humble opinion on a wide range of subjects from aliens to zits.

0-345-46461-3 • 8" x 8" • 128 pages
$12.95 / $17.95 CAN • Ballantine Trade Paperback

IN DOG YEARS I'D BE DEAD Garfield at 25

Experience twenty-five years of the furry phenomenon known as Garfield with this fun, in-depth, and lavishly illustrated book.

0-345-45204-6 • 9" x 11⅞" • 224 pages
$19.95 / $27.95 CAN • Ballantine Trade Paperback

GARFIELD'S BOOK OF CAT NAMES

Garfield, the first name in fun, offers the definitive guide to giving your cat a memorable moniker in this new-and-improved colorful classic.

0-345-48516-5 • 5½" x 6" • 96 pages
$10.95 / $15.95 CAN • Ballantine Trade Paperback

Check out all the Garfield books on www.garfield.com